Praise for *Inside the Minds*

"A rare peek behind the curtains and into the minds of the industry's best." - Brandon Baum, Partner, Cooley Godward

"Tremendous insights...a must read..." - James Quinn, Litigation Chair, Weil, Gotshal & Manges

"Unlike any other business book..." - Bruce Keller, IP Litigation Chair, Debevoise & Plimpton

"Intensely personal, practical advice from seasoned dealmakers." - Mary Ann Jorgenson, Coordinator of Business Practice Area, Squire, Sanders & Dempsey

"An informative insider's perspective..." - Gary Klotz, Labor Chair, Butzel Long

"A must read..." - Raymond Wheeler, Labor Chair, Morrison & Foerster

"Great practical advice and thoughtful insights." - Mark Gruhin, Partner, Schmeltzer, Aptaker & Shepard, P.C.

"A compilation of thoughts, insights and tips from some of the leading labor lawyers in America...." - Michael Reynvaan, Labor Chair, Perkins Coie

"Great information for business executives and employers of any size." - Judy Langevin, Employment Chair, Gray, Plant, Mooty, Mooty & Bennett

"Useful and understandable insight..." - Stuart Lubitz, Partner, Hogan & Hartson, Co-Head of Litigation, Simpson Thacher & Bartlett

"A valuable probe into the thought, perspectives, and techniques of accomplished professionals...the authors place their endeavors in a context rarely gleaned from text books or treatises." - Charles Birenbaum, Labor Chair, Thelen Reid & Priest

"A snapshot of everything you need..." - Charles Koob, Co-Head of Litigation Department, Simpson Thacher & Bartle

www.Aspatore.com

Aspatore Books is the largest and most exclusive publisher of C-Level executives (CEO, CFO, CTO, CMO, Partner) from the world's most respected companies. Aspatore annually publishes C-Level executives from over half the Global 500, top 250 professional services firms, law firms (MPs/Chairs), and other leading companies of all sizes. By focusing on publishing only C-Level executives, Aspatore provides professionals of all levels with proven business intelligence from industry insiders, rather than relying on the knowledge of unknown authors and analysts. Aspatore Books is committed to publishing a highly innovative line of business books, redefining and expanding the meaning of such books as indispensable resources for professionals of all levels. In addition to individual best-selling business titles, Aspatore Books publishes the following unique lines of business books: Inside the Minds, Business Bibles, Bigwig Briefs, C-Level Business Review (Quarterly), Book Binders, ExecRecs, and The C-Level Test, innovative resources for all professionals. Aspatore is a privately held company headquartered in Boston, Massachusetts, with employees around the world.

Inside the Minds

The critically acclaimed *Inside the Minds* series provides readers of all levels with proven business intelligence from C-Level executives (CEO, CFO, CTO, CMO, Partner) from the world's most respected companies. Each chapter is comparable to a white paper or essay and is a future-oriented look at where an industry/profession/topic is heading and the most important issues for future success. Each author has been carefully chosen through an exhaustive selection process by the *Inside the Minds* editorial board to write a chapter for this book. *Inside the Minds* was conceived in order to give readers actual insights into the leading minds of business executives worldwide. Because so few books or other publications are actually written by executives in industry, *Inside the Minds* presents an unprecedented look at various industries and professions never before available.

INSIDE THE MINDS

Wireless Leadership Strategies

*Industry Insiders on Cutting Costs and Growing Profits
While Staying Customer-Focused*

BOOK IDEA SUBMISSIONS

If you are a C-Level executive or senior lawyer interested in submitting a book idea or manuscript to the Aspatore editorial board, please e-mail jason@aspatore.com. Aspatore is especially looking for highly specific book ideas that would have a direct financial impact on behalf of a reader. Completed books can range from 20 to 2,000 pages – the topic and "need to read" aspect of the material are most important, not the length. Include your book idea, biography, and any additional pertinent information.

Published by Aspatore, Inc.

For corrections, company/title updates, comments or any other inquiries please e-mail info@aspatore.com.

First Printing, 2005
10 9 8 7 6 5 4 3 2 1

Copyright © 2005 by Aspatore, Inc. All rights reserved. Printed in the United States of America. No part of this publication may be reproduced or distributed in any form or by any means, or stored in a database or retrieval system, except as permitted under Sections 107 or 108 of the United States Copyright Act, without prior written permission of the publisher.

ISBN 1-59622-063-5 Library of Congress Control Number: 2005925427

Inside the Minds Managing Editor, Kari A. Russ, Edited by Marissa Berenson.

Material in this book is for educational purposes only. This book is sold with the understanding that neither any of the authors or the publisher is engaged in rendering legal, accounting, investment, or any other professional service. Neither the publisher nor the authors assume any liability for any errors or omissions or for how this book or its contents are used or interpreted or for any consequences resulting directly or indirectly from the use of this book. For legal advice, please consult your personal lawyer.

This book is printed on acid free paper.

A special thanks to all the individuals who made this book possible.

The views expressed by the individuals in this book (or the individuals on the cover) do not necessarily reflect the views shared by the companies they are employed by (or the companies mentioned in this book). The employment status and affiliations of authors with the companies referenced are subject to change.

Wireless Leadership Strategies

Industry Insiders on Cutting Costs and Growing Profits While Staying Customer-Focused

CONTENTS

Robert J. Laikin   7
THE FUTURE OF WIRELESS TECHNOLOGIES

Jim Taiclet   23
A STRATEGY OF SMART GROWTH, OPERATIONAL EXCELLENCE, AND OPTIMIZED FINANCING

John Elms   39
THE EVER-GROWING WIRELESS INDUSTRY

Jim Grady   53
DEVELOPING HIGH-VALUE SOLUTIONS FOR WIRELESS CARRIERS

Michael Z. Jones   63
WIRELESS SALES STRATEGIES

Michael A. Grollman   85
STRIKING THE RIGHT BALANCE IN THE WIRELESS INDUSTRY

Todd Myers 95
DEVELOPING WI-FI

Ken Cranston 103
SUCCESSFULLY RIDING THE TECHNOLOGY WAVE

Greg Murphy 113
MANAGING A WIRELESS NETWORK

The Future of Wireless Technologies

Robert J. Laikin
Chairman of the Board & Chief Executive Officer
Brightpoint, Inc.

A Vision of Future Changes

The wireless device market has always been changing rapidly and has become very dynamic and competitive. Newer technologies drive the replacement cycle for wireless devices, which, in turn, fuels the demand for these devices. Third Generation (3G) technologies and other emerging complimentary technologies, such as Wi-Fi and WiMAX, are driving the demand for converged wireless devices, such as Smartphones, Pocket PC Editions, Palm Treo, RIM's Blackberry and Wi-Fi enabled wireless phones, which combine video, voice and data features.

Brightpoint, Inc. has the talent, the financial strength and the infrastructure in place to take advantage of the above factors. The replacement and upgrade cycle remain as the single largest factor fueling the demand within the wireless portable device market. Newer technologies and associated features and applications are key reasons for the increasingly shortened replacement cycle. In certain countries, for example, in Western Europe, wireless penetration has reached more than 90 percent of the population. In Taiwan and Israel, it has gone so far as to reach 100 percent of the population, which means that almost every unit sold in these countries is a replacement unit.

Other exciting growth opportunities in the wireless industry include Wireless LAN or Wi-Fi, the proliferation of Advanced Wireless Devices (or Smart devices) and Wireless Data Services, especially Mobile Entertainment Content such as music, games, ringtones and wallpapers. Based on a study by UMTS (Universal Mobile Telecommunications System) Forum, mobile intranet and extranet access by enterprise customers and customized infotainment by end-users will become the dominant wireless data services. Market research estimates that by 2009, mobile gaming services in the U.S. alone will generate $1.8 billion annually, which is approximately 4.4 percent of total wireless data revenues. Mobile gaming will continue its rise as a key contributor to wireless data usage and global revenues. As part of our growth strategy, we are expanding our products and offerings by adding compelling value-added services to our portfolio.

The promise of Broadband is changing the wireless industry, as we know it today, by offering a technology that can deliver video, voice and data or 'triple play' services in entirely new ways over interactive and integrated wireless networks. The wireless industry is moving toward a subscriber environment, which is always connected and in which the end-user will have seamless access to the necessary bandwidth. More consumers and households are using Broadband for Internet access than ever before. The deployment of 3G infrastructure and both WLAN and WWAN technologies are further fueling the replacement cycle and the wireless handset demand on a global basis.

Based on industry reports, CDMA2000 achieved a major milestone in the second quarter of 2004 by surpassing 100 million users worldwide. It is forecasted that the CDMA2000 base will reach 290 million users by 2008. Based on industry reports, it is expected that approximately 18 to 20 million WCDMA handsets will have been sold globally in 2004. Wireless network operators around the world are looking to drive their Average Revenue Per Users (ARPUs) and revenues via innovative services. I look forward to Brightpoint's participation in providing these new services, such as Mobile Content and Smart Device Solutions, and will continue to help our customers succeed. Differentiation and accommodating the customer are key necessary factors if companies are going to succeed. They must be flexible, cost efficient and highly service-oriented to create a winning formula.

A Different Approach

The foundation of our strategy is built around customer commitment and making our customer's success our primary business focus. Flexible business models with customized services, combined with a talent pool of industry veterans, differentiates Brightpoint from other companies. No other company in the industry matches the breadth of wireless device distribution and customized services offered by Brightpoint on a global basis. Brightpoint moves wireless devices into the hands of subscribers on behalf of mobile phone companies, such as Nextel, Virgin Mobile, Vodafone and TracFone, and on behalf of manufacturers such as Nokia, Sony Ericsson, LG, Motorola and Samsung. In 2003, our global operations handled or touched more than 20 million wireless devices. Our global revenue that year was $1.8 billion dollars.

We move large quantities of wireless devices, primarily wireless cell phones, through two distinct and very different business units. Roughly half of our units are sold through our distribution business. In this area, we act as a wholesale distributor for Nokia, Samsung, LG, Motorola and other leading manufacturers. We offer traditional distribution services, such as same day shipping and credit terms. In this business, we sell to mobile network operators, retailers and authorized wireless agents. The other half of our units are handled through our logistics services business. In this area, we provide services such as warehousing, software loading, packaging, fulfillment, credit, billing and collection services; call centers and Web site hosting. This is a fee-based business that provides services to leading wireless network operators and mobile virtual network operators (MVNOs), such as Nextel, Sprint PCS, Virgin Mobile, Vodafone, Cricket, TracFone and MetroPCS.

With our extensive experience working with leading MVNOs, such as Virgin Mobile, TracFone and Boost, Brightpoint is well positioned to address many future opportunities as MVNOs proliferate and continue to outsource mission critical functions. This is positive for Brightpoint, as it will further increase our addressable market. Today, we have over 1,100 global employees working in eighteen locations across fourteen countries, and we service approximately 20,000 customers.

Selecting a Product Mix and Handling the Competition

The correct product mix is determined primarily as a function of our business and marketing strategy. Our business strategy dictates a certain mix of low-, mid- and high-tier products to achieve a desired financial result. Our specific marketing strategy, then, is formulated to support the desired business strategy. Our business and marketing strategy is enhanced by our extensive knowledge of the marketplace and of the wants and needs of our customer base.

Brightpoint, as a customer-oriented and committed company, must begin with the marketplace and then align our business strategies and organization to meet market demands. Adding or losing products is a function of the needs and wants of the marketplace. Advances in technology will change the requirements of the end-users, and that drives the desired product mix shift within our company. Competitive pressures are also compelling factors driving the product mix shift strategies in our company. The need to differentiate Brightpoint from its competitors is one of the key success factors in acquiring, managing and retaining our customer base. Once again, this drives our product mix.

The supplier and customer relationship is of the utmost importance in order for Brightpoint to grow and retain our market share within a particular region. Creative marketing strategies in support of our suppliers and customers drive the demand for the products we sell. In turn, this helps grow our market share in the regions in which we operate. As a company, Brightpoint is focused on making supplier and customer success our business. Meeting and exceeding customers' expectations enhances our relationship with them. Because of the efficiencies built around our operational, financial and marketing processes, we believe that we are able to outperform our competition. Differentiating our services and value proposition to our customers and suppliers positions Brightpoint advantageously in the wireless distribution and logistics value chain.

Customer Service

The performances of all Brightpoint employees are, directly or indirectly, measured based upon customer service and commitment. The foundation of Brightpoint was built around the customer's principal role, and it continues to be our guiding force. Our brand slogan, "Your Success Is Our Business," reflects our commitment to customers and stakeholders. Making sure that we do what we say and say what we do is one way of meeting and exceeding customer expectations. We listen to our customers and consider their feedback and suggestions very seriously. We have extensive customer commitment measurement programs in place to ensure that we continue to receive their feedback on our products and services.

Brightpoint's customer-centric attitude is reflected in the actions of our employees around the world. We are flexible, and, therefore, we are able to offer customized services to optimize our customers' requirements. Brightpoint continues to invest in infrastructure and IT systems to ensure low cost, quality, accurate and timely delivery of our services to our customers and products on behalf of our vendors. Trust is another very important word in our dictionary. Our vendors and customers trust Brightpoint to implement their plans, and the Brightpoint team works relentlessly to ensure that we maintain that trust and never let our vendors and customers down.

Facing Challenges in the Wireless Industry

The wireless communications industry is largely a spin-off of the wire-line telecom industry. Many of the existing wireless network operators were once landline phone companies. As wireless first emerged in the 1980s, Brightpoint dealt with the frequent desire by wireless network operators to in-source all of the functions to support their businesses. During the '80s, the average monthly cost of a wireless phone bill was $200 for airtime, and a handset could cost as much as $5,000. As a result, sales volumes were very low initially. There were only a few manufacturers of wireless handsets. Companies like Oki Telecom, Panasonic and Mitsubishi were prominent manufacturers. Nokia and Ericsson were lesser-known names in those days. Many companies in the wireless industry were making substantial margins and, therefore, did not want to listen to alternative distribution and product handling strategies.

As competition among wireless network operators increased in the late '80s and early '90s, and as the PCS/Second Generation (2G) licenses were issued, many wireless markets went from having one or two known wireless carriers to today's figure of many more carriers in certain markets. Brightpoint was able to show eager audiences new, innovative services that could make a wireless network operator more competitive. At the same time, airtime costs dropped dramatically, as did the cost of hardware. Battery life on handheld phones increased from a maximum of two hours to an entire day. The consumers' demand for wireless phones and services exploded, and those changes have helped us overcome many difficulties we faced ten to twenty years ago.

The ever-changing dynamic nature of the wireless industry and the dynamic nature of our suppliers' and customers' business models are, currently, the most challenging parts of our business. Our position in the value chain, although unique and valuable, leaves us, to a certain extent, dependent upon the plans of our customers and suppliers. If there are price wars in the marketplace, Brightpoint must adapt rather quickly and focus on other variables to beat the competition and grow profitably. If there is a change in the strategic direction of one of our key customers, we must be ready to change our course seamlessly and adopt a direction in support of that customer. The business mix shift between our two distinct lines of businesses can pose challenging issues for us with respect to revenue growth and profitability. Regional differences and variation in business models by region or country, while interesting, continue to challenge us on a regular basis.

Measuring Success

Enhancing long-term shareholder value is the reason why we have developed our strategy, and we also use shareholder value as a way to measure our success. Financial success is measured in terms of meeting or exceeding our financial plan and metrics. Operational success is measured in terms of productivity gains' and efficiency gains in our operational processes. Strategic success is achieved by successfully achieving our planned objectives. All of these successes must, ultimately, enhance long-term shareholder value, and that becomes a critical measurement of Brightpoint's success. Brightpoint's success also depends on customer satisfaction and employee satisfaction. We measure success based on how satisfied our customers are with our products and services and how happy our employees are delivering those products and services to our customers. Our ability to attract and retain highly skilled talent is an important measure of our success.

Golden Rules for Wireless Industry Success

- Remain steadfastly committed to customer and supplier relationships;
- Provide low cost, high quality and customized service options;
- Maintain a disciplined approach to financial models and the balance sheet.

Position Goals

Some of the other areas I focus on as CEO are the key supplier and customer relationships. I spend much of my time working with key suppliers at all levels and on a global basis. They may be existing suppliers, potential suppliers, customers or, as the regions request, the corporate group. I work to assist them with, or offer guidance about, any new business development opportunities they might have.

I also work with the executive management team to build the corporate image and brand equity with investors and industry media. This may include events like investor conferences, trade shows or media days. We take the results that regions provide for the company and arrange them into a concise presentation that can be presented to Wall Street, suppliers or banks. The purpose is to communicate who Brightpoint is, our marketing position and story.

Because we are a public company, based on new Sarbanes-Oxley requirements, I work with the general counsel, as well as the CFO, as necessary.

A Collaborative Approach

My position requires cooperation with many different contingents. I work closely with the CFO. I also work with our three regional presidents: the president of the Americas, the president of Europe, and the president of Asia/Pacific. I have a direct working relationship with each of these executives.

I also work with Anurag Gupta, senior vice president of global strategy; I work closely with our senior vice president of human resources in areas that involve various HR strategies and issues that arise from time to time, as well as strategic initiatives. Lastly, as the key communicator with the Board of Directors, I work regularly on Board-related and strategic issues. If I were to estimate where my time is spent, I would say one-third involves working with the Board of Directors, one-third is spent with the regional presidents as a group and the remaining third of my time is filled working with the remaining areas.

Planning for Growth

To set a company growth plan for each year, we examine how fast the industry is growing. We look at our market position; the condition of our balance sheet, and the various markets that we believe will be long-term, profitable markets. Then we assemble growth targets to determine what is reasonable. Our goal is to grow faster than the market grows, and the only way to do that is to take market share. We work very closely with existing customers and new players in order to gauge our customers' growth and expand with them. If we accomplish that, we can increase the efficiency of their systems and processes.

I am also the head of a strategy development process, which I formulate by working very closely with Anurag Gupta. It is a collaborative global strategy path as opposed to a top-down dictatorship, and the shared process builds on the marketing opportunities of different regions. We firmly believe that market opportunities dictate global growth strategies, and therefore we take the market input requirements and incorporate them into our global strategy. Because we want a flawless execution of these global strategic elements on a regional basis, we measure milestones with the executive team on a periodic basis. Not only do we spend time developing our growth strategy plan, but we also allot enough time to ensuring that all is executed according to the plan. Any strategy is only as good as its execution.

Our corporate directional strategy is growth. Our global growth strategic elements include geographic expansion, transferring and expanding our products and service offerings from one Brightpoint geographic region to another, which leverages our core competence and skill base, adding new products and services to our portfolio to enhance our value proposition to our customers, and building and promoting our brand equity consistently across the wireless industry. Our regional growth plans are aligned to our global strategy. This ensures the effective and efficient allocation of resources throughout the company.

Our growth plans are not isolated, but rather they support and are supported by the growth plans of our suppliers and customers. We are selective in our expansion plans and do not believe in growing only for the sake of growing. Using a robust process, we develop our operating plans on a yearly basis and align them to our strategic initiatives globally. Execution is key to ensuring the flawless implementation of our growth plans. Therefore, our employees around the world are focused on execution. Communication is essential to making sure that all our employees understand our strategies and plans. We have strong communication strategies in place at all levels of our organization to ensure clear delivery of our priorities on a quarterly basis. Continuous Productivity Improvement Teams are in effect in all regions, driving synergies and streamlining processes to improve our cost effectiveness.

Measurements and accountability are two key behaviors that I continue to promote throughout the company. Our company culture is built around the concept of "rewards for results." I believe results are the ultimate measure of how well a company has executed on its plans. You must ask whether you achieved what you set out to do. In our case, measurement criteria are set in advance annually for all of our plans and strategic initiatives. Each initiative has someone who will ultimately be accountable for the success or failure of that initiative. Timely accomplishment of major milestones is the mechanism we use to track progress on a quarterly basis. Performance evaluations at the end of each year take stock of the successes and failures of our plans and initiatives. You have to keep accountability in the forefront if you want flawless execution. Execution is the key to enhancing long-term shareholder value.

Increasing Revenue

We have developed a strategic plan to find ways of growing geographically into certain markets and, therefore, increasing revenue. Additionally, we continually ask ourselves whether we should add new products or services in order to increase revenue.

To use the example of our industry, if Smart devices are going to be the focus for the next several years, then we must determine with whom we will align in both the hardware and content realms. We also need enterprise opportunities, because Smart phones for a business user will need to be installed behind a firewall at the enterprise level. Each of those interrelated prospects may contribute to Brightpoint's growth. Because we are located in numerous countries, we offer different services in different markets. We are still in the process of moving what works in Australia to France, or what works in Sweden to the U.S. Some examples of these services are prepaid airtime programs and Smart phone logistics, which have experienced success in certain markets and will be rolled out elsewhere.

Reducing Expenses

We continually focus on reducing expenses. We look at how a market is performing and determine the appropriate action. We examined our corporate expenses and made some tough decisions about eliminating positions. In certain areas, we outsourced positions and jobs because we felt they could be addressed more affordably. Along with our worldwide financial departments and executives, we approached the challenge together and sought ideas for reducing company-wide expenses. Most of all, we managed and balanced changes globally, rather than focusing only on one particular area.

In certain markets, we wanted to continue to invest and grow for the future. In others, for example, some of the more mature markets, we felt as if we had the ability to reduce expenses more heavily. If we had three people in the marketing department, we reviewed it as a team and decided we could operate effectively and efficiently with one person. We realized in certain areas we could leverage a key position among five countries, rather than have one in each country. Reducing expenses requires tough decisions, and it is not an easy thing to do.

Recovering from the Loss of Talent

Over the years, we have experienced occasions when we've lost certain employees. When that happens, we have succession plans in place at all levels of the organization to help us fill the position(s). If an internal replacement is not possible, we go through a recruitment process, led by our human resources team.

We have a core group of people who have been together on the team for quite some time. All the same, our company has had its ups and downs. In the '90s, we were one of the fastest-growing public companies in our industry, and, in early 2000, we suffered through restructuring and downsizing. Our viability was tested, and the team made it through that rough time. In recent years, we brought in a number of talented people, such as Frank Terence (EVP and CFO), Anurag Gupta (SVP global strategy), Lisa Kelley (SVP and corporate controller), Annette Cyr (SVP HR), and Anthony Mackle (VP internal audit).

Five Skills of a Successful CEO

If I were to pinpoint five of the most important skills a CEO can and must possess, the first of these would be the ability to communicate well. The CEO has to be able to communicate important priorities and messages to all of the stakeholders. Effective communication of the company's vision and strategy sets the tone for the entire organization. It helps in aligning everybody's goals to the corporate objectives in a cohesive fashion.

At Brightpoint, I send out a monthly CEO message, via e-mail, to a majority of the employees. Every month, I choose a different topic to discuss. Sometimes it may be business related, and, at times, it is about work-life balance. This e-mail is sent to more than 1100 global employees, and I encourage their feedback. Last month we chose a topic that asked the employee, "Describe your role" and "Tell me about yourself." I received about a 95 percent response rate from people in fourteen different countries, and I personally replied to all of the e-mails. I was told about different cultural issues, heard various stories and passions and read about individuals' commitments. The positive responses I received were incredible, and it demonstrated the pride of the people working for Brightpoint and just how much they love their jobs and Brightpoint's missions. It was one of the most rewarding projects I have ever done because of the feedback I acquired. It is very important for a CEO to constantly find ways to extend the invitation of open communication.

A second important skill for a CEO is obtaining a thorough vision and understanding of your industry. I have been in the industry since its inception. Although I am forty-one years old, I have worked in this industry for nearly twenty years. I talk to and work with Wall Street telecom analyst investors. I attend trade shows. I discuss global strategy for the industry with the manufacturing leaders and the network operator leaders. The CEO must continually read and educate himself or herself, as well as educate the executive team. Also, part of knowing the industry is having good working relationships with most of the major players in the space.

Thirdly, a successful CEO must have a good basic understanding of finances and know his or her way around a balance sheet. He or she must have a solid understanding of what financial needs may arise depending upon market conditions. The CEO has to know which financial metrics are important to the company's shareholders.

A financial understanding leads to a fourth ability of successful CEOs, and that is to communicate well with investment bankers and analysts and shareholders' investors.

Our company went public in 1994. We had subsequent stock offerings in 1995 and 1997. We also issued debt in the form of convertible notes in 1998. We then went through a re-negotiation with our bondholders in 2002 in relation to certain terms and conditions that resulted in our repurchase of the bonds at that time, as well as in 2003. During that period, I spent a lot of time raising money in the public markets, and I was able to ask what was important to shareholders and analysts and others on Wall Street and discovered what could differentiate us from a competitor in the investment decision process. I heard and understood what was important to them, whether it was international growth, growth of a logistics-based business or a focus on distribution.

When the PCS/2G players arrived in the '90s, airtime competition increased, and wireless network operators had to differentiate their services and offerings, giving Brightpoint the ability to branch into the logistics area. We transformed from simply a distributor to a logistics provider and distributor. Today a wireless phone is an extension of the Internet. It has an MP3 player built in it and, in certain circumstances, requires a business user to go behind a firewall at the enterprise level. There are entertainment services, such as gaming, ringtones, ringback tones and e-mail. With the incorporation of all the other services that accompany the high-speed wireless network, the industry has become more complicated. Those products and Smart devices require more customization, and we must continue to change our service offerings and address new developments or, at times, a completely different market. We must keep adapting and changing our business, determining who we are and what we do on the basis of where the market is going.

Smart devices are sold in many countries today. A figure of 50,000 sold in a small or medium-sized country would indicate a substantial month for Smart devices, and, within five years, they may comprise a larger percentage of the market. Devices will very likely open your garage door, and they may be the e-money used to pay your banking services, and a button on your phone will allow you to go through a turnstile at the movies or purchase a Coke from a vending machine. In some markets today, a parking meter is paid when a button on a wireless device subtracts the payment from one's checking account. Remote monitoring is popular in Europe. If you are away from a summer home, you can place a video camera there and access the signal in the video feed through your cell phone.

There are many exciting new services that are emerging in our industry, and Brightpoint needs to be able to adapt and change as voice merges with data and content. Our success will hinge on our ability to adapt. As CEO, I must ensure our people are not focused only on short-term objectives, but are also thinking about where the industry is going to be in the long-term. Together, we need to provide the services and pave the road before the cars arrive. In the logistics area, we did that successfully and were able to build capacity before there was tremendous demand. But we must always be positioned properly in anticipation of the next stage of our industry. A CEO's list of important skills will always be changing, but it has not changed drastically in the past few years. A crucial talent may be added or removed from the list, but, at the moment, those are the essential five qualities for a successful CEO in our industry.

Balancing Work and Life

Keeping one's personal outside of work life and work balanced can be difficult in the wireless industry, because that very technology has made it much easier to be continuously connected to your work. Wireless phones and e-mail access make it seem as if one's personal life and work are paralleled. At Brightpoint, we try to stress the importance of balance to our employees because, if work time is too dominant, something will inevitably go wrong. I can say from personal experience that this is not always easy to do. We try to achieve balance, but we must continue to try harder. There are paid time off programs for everyone in the company, and we urge people to take this time and attempt to reach equilibrium by trying not to work extremely long hours. To be effective, passionate and result-oriented, one must rejuvenate him or herself on a regular basis. You must give time to your family because there is an argument that we work hard so we can provide the best we can for our family. Family is certainly a motivating factor, and keeping work time balanced with your family time helps ensure productivity on a long-term basis.

Setting Goals and Guiding the Execution

We have a planning process, which leads up to an annual operating plan. The operating plan must be aligned to our overall global Corporate Strategy. Our regional presidents and CFOs, working in tandem with our corporate finance team, develop the annual operating plan. This becomes our guiding light for the year. Through monthly calls, we are able to track, by country, whether we are on track and what we can do to meet and exceed the plan. Each country is represented on these calls by its senior management team. They provide us with an update on the wireless market in their regions, what is driving sales and where the bottlenecks are. Operational, marketing, business and financial issues and concerns are discussed on these calls. In addition, I make a monthly global call to the key leadership of the company, including regional presidents and country MDs. In these calls, I outline our vision and strategy and disseminate my thoughts on the industry. Sharing information on the industry and discussing regional concerns helps our team resolve the issues in an efficient and expedient fashion. It allows for cross-pollination at the senior level and drives business development.

Robert J. Laikin, founder of Brightpoint, Inc., has been a director of the company since its inception in August 1989. Mr. Laikin has been chairman of the board and chief executive officer of the company since January 1994. Mr. Laikin was president of the company from June 1992 until September 1996 and vice president and treasurer of the company from August 1989 until May 1992. From July 1986 to December 1987, Mr. Laikin was vice president, and from January 1988 to February 1993, president of

Century Cellular Network, Inc., a company engaged in the retail sale of cellular telephones and accessories.

Dedication: *To my parents, Judy and Sid Laikin, for their unconditional love and support.*

A Strategy of Smart Growth, Operational Excellence, and Optimized Financing

Jim Taiclet
CEO
American Tower

Wireless and Telecom Leadership Strategies

Our company, American Tower, is the leading provider of critical infrastructure to the wireless and broadcast industries in the United States, Mexico, and Brazil. We own, operate and manage real estate, tower structures and building rooftops used by wireless carriers, such as Cingular and Verizon, and by television and radio stations to transmit their signals. Our company's mission is to enable the fast and efficient deployment of advanced wireless and broadcast services. We accomplish this by placing multiple carriers or broadcasters on a single tower, which also benefits the communities in which we operate, since fewer towers are then needed to provide these services.

At American Tower, our vision is that, in the future, an increasing proportion of telecommunications is going to be wireless. Consumer and business desire for the freedom offered by mobility in communications will drive migration from wired phones and wired data devices to wireless phones and wireless data devices. This migration of wireless is occurring at a reasonably high pace, and, since the base of wire line telephony is so large, this migration will continue over a number of years.

Our company is very focused on this anticipated wireless industry growth. We believe wireless growth is going to be robust and fairly steady, without dramatic fluctuations. We also believe this is beneficial to our company because it should result in a sustained, stable rate of growth into the future.

As the leading operator of tower assets, we don't have great swings in either our revenue or profitability; it is a fairly steadily growing business. As wireless carriers add more subscribers to their services and as those people use wireless devices more and more as their communications vehicles, demand on wireless networks increases, and, therefore, there is greater need for infrastructure, the towers or rooftops where antennas can be placed to transmit the required signal.

In order to succeed in the wireless industry, carriers need to be leaders in understanding how people want to use wireless and how to encourage people to use wireless and un-tether from their wired lines, whether it is a phone line at home, a phone line at work or a data line into your computer.

Carriers that understand the end customer best and develop products and services for the individual subscriber that are easy to use and complimentary to a more mobile personal or work lifestyle are going to be successful.

The technology is available to drive the demand today. The driving factor is how a carrier makes its service offering compelling for the individual end user to either sign onto a new service or increase the proportion of his or her current services towards wireless.

Three Strategies to Creating Value

Our industry sector, represented by the five publicly-traded tower companies, manages a substantial portion of the tower assets located in the U.S. At American Tower, we are in the number one scale position with approximately 15,000 towers. Our main growth engine is to add customers, in the form of wireless cell sites and broadcast antennas, onto the towers we own and operate. In addition, we build around 100 new towers sites each year.

Our company built its current base of assets by purchasing tower portfolios from carriers such as Verizon, Alltel, and AT&T; acquiring smaller tower companies and by building a significant number of towers from 1999 to 2001. Going forward, our company is executing a three pronged strategy. The first element of our strategy is to strive to add to our scale but in a 'smart' manner. In other words, don't overpay for assets. We are also seeking merger and acquisition opportunities regularly. However, we are not in a position where we have to pay an excessive price to acquire a company, whether it owns five towers or 5,000 towers, because we already have the scale to be successful. So, seeking growth at reasonable prices is our first strategy to build toward the future.

The second element of our strategy is to be a great operator of tower assets, which simply comes down to the blocking and tackling of managing any business. Our particular industry is only eight years old and was formed around the time of the PCS auctions in the mid-1990s to serve a market that expanded from just two wireless carriers to, suddenly, six or seven per market. It would have been inefficient for all those carriers to have their own sets of individual towers. Thus, the tower industry was created to enable the rapid launch and development of competitive, advanced wireless services in the U.S., using the new licenses that were awarded. Sharable infrastructure was essential for the creation of the wireless industry that exists today, which is what our company provides.

To improve our performance, we are introducing and advancing, in our own company, best operating management practices that have been used successfully by much more mature companies over a long period of time. We are streamlining those practices and bringing them online. Our operational initiatives are in three major areas. The first is talent management, in which we identify, rate, and determine the growth opportunities that should be afforded to our key people throughout the organization. Twice each year, I conduct a formal review of all of the management teams in the company. Each executive and manager is rated in terms of performance (tangible results) and behavior (how the results were accomplished). High potential individuals are identified for professional development and advancement. In addition, anyone who is not performing or behaving up to the desired standards is also identified. These talent management reviews drive a performance culture and reward those who make a special contribution to the company's success. Another key output of these reviews is a comprehensive, current succession plan for each executive and management position in the company.

The second operational initiative, performance management, comes in the form of very specific goals and objectives that start with me and cascade down through the 120 managers in the company. They are all interlinked, so that managers in different functions and locations are fully coordinated. The goals and objectives are also tangible and quantitative, and they tie directly to compensation. The goals and objectives cover four categories and are tailored to each individual's role. The categories include customer satisfaction, financial performance, people development and operational results/improvement. The goals and objectives for the company, myself and the senior management team are communicated directly in our annual management meetings. Thereafter, each manager agrees on his or her own set of goals and objectives with his or her supervisor.

Our third area of operational focus is continuous process improvement. We have a dedicated team that works throughout the business to map our processes, and we use statistically-based analytical tools to improve the quality and speed of each process. We are specifically focused on processes that directly connect with our customers. For example, I am very excited about a project completed recently to enhance the speed and accuracy of sales information to our customer, called Fast Track. The project will ease and quicken our customers' own processes of making buying decisions to go on one of our towers. So, it is these three initiatives—talent management, performance management and process improvement—that we are using to address our second strategy of operational excellence.

Since we are an asset-based company, the third element of our strategy is to continue to strive to get the most effective financing possible. That means aggressive balance-sheet management, refinancing when rates are favorable, paying down debt judiciously with our free cash flow and deciding when we may consider buying back shares or initiating a dividend program for our shareholders at some point in the future.

Profit Growth

Our 15,000 sites in the U.S., Mexico, and Brazil are more numerous than any company in our industry. We have what we consider franchise locations, and each of these towers, typically, does not have another competing site within a half a mile. If a carrier needs a new cell site in a given location, odds are there is no other choice but ours if an American Tower site is located there. Location is the most important attribute for profit growth. We have the greatest number of franchises and, therefore, our industry-leading scale is our most important profit driver.

The second way for us to grow profit is through speed and customer service. We want to work very quickly in providing a set of complex information—what I call "second-order data"—to our customers to make buying decisions. There are a number of criteria, such as zoning approvals, building permits and structural analysis of the tower, to determine whether a new customer can add another set of equipment to the tower. All of these criteria require some level of research. The tower company to get information back to the customer most rapidly (and accurately) is likely to get additional market share. In a situation where there might be another choice for a tower, we want to be the one that gets the fastest and most reliable information to the customer, in order to win the business.

The third driver of profitability is continuously advancing the customer relationship from the top level throughout the organization, so that people know each other at every level and are comfortable working together and sharing information. We have structured our company to be customer focused. The general managers of our seven marketing areas in the U.S., Mexico, and Brazil are our senior local business leaders. They are responsible for customer relationships, sales and the full P&L. Each has a dedicated sales manager and sales team to ensure that we have local contacts for our customers throughout the country. In addition, the first category in an area manager's goals and objectives (and, as a consequence, his or her compensation) is customer relations. It is also the first category of my own goals and objectives, as well as for the respective presidents of our U.S. and International divisions. The three of us build customer relationships at the corporate level with our major customers.

Challenges in the Industry

One of the most significant challenges for our business is dealing with complexity and massive amounts of data, as we have 15,000 separate communications sites and, therefore, 15,000 individual P&Ls. With great attention to detail, you can maximize every single revenue opportunity for each of those 15,000 P&Ls. You must also be very cost-conscious of each one of those tower sites and determine ways to reduce costs at the same time that you are adding revenue.

Fundamentally, we operate within a great business model. We can add revenue without adding costs, since cost is associated with the tower structure and the revenue is associated with cell sites, which are simply sets of equipment that a customer puts on that tower. Our cost does not necessarily increase when a customer adds to a tower we already have in operation. Over the past three years, we have added about $200 million of annualized revenue over with zero increase in cooperating cost. As a result, the company has consistently been averaging 90 to 100 percent of incremental revenue flowing through to operating profit. As we move forward into the future, our greatest area of opportunity is to maximize the growth of free cash flow by securing every single lease that is available to us and by reducing every dollar of cost that we can along the way.

Picking Your Product

Three years ago, only 39 percent of our revenue came from the tower leasing business. Previously, most of the company's revenue came from more volatile, lower-margin, more unpredictable type businesses, which were below scale in a less than favorable economic environment. These businesses were susceptible to changes in the economy and were not based on long-term leases. In late 2001, our company's founder and our management team decided to focus exclusively on the tower leasing business and divest the units in our other business segments.

We sold our lower-margin businesses to companies that had greater scale in each relevant area and reinvested those proceeds into higher-margin tower assets in our leasing divisions. For example, we had a steel manufacturing business so we could make the steel structures for our broadcast towers. We also had a lighting business for the red flashing lights you see on the tower. We were a manufacturing business, but we were below scale, so we sold those manufacturing businesses to a larger scale manufacturing company that has the size and expertise to be successful throughout the business cycle. After selling these manufacturing businesses, we purchased additional towers with those proceeds. And, for the most part, our employees in our divested business units transferred to the acquiring company. Preserving jobs in the transition to new ownership was one of the major objectives in divesting these units to new parents.

In our portfolio assessment approach, we assessed every business we had in our corporation to see if it had the basic attributes to be successful by asking some key questions. Do we have the management talent and depth in place to compete? Do we have a scale or other competitive advantage so that we can continue to be increasingly successful over time, or are we facing any fundamental disadvantages?

Turning back to our customers, it takes a lot to finance the tower leasing business model at sufficient scale. We have $5 billion worth of assets being managed with an organization of 700 knowledgeable, talented people. We have the scale, and we have the people that know how to run a multinational communications infrastructure operation. In our portfolio assessment, we determined that we also had the customer relationships and regulatory experience that provided competitive advantages in the tower leasing business.

Keeping Ahead of the Competition and Abreast of Technology

Our competing product is not usually another tower company's site, but it is the alternative for our customers to build their own new towers. Our company offers the option of "co-location," which is simply putting a customer's equipment on our existing tower. In almost every case, it is much faster, simpler and easier for wireless carriers and broadcasters to co-locate on our tower than to build their own new structures.

We also operate in an environment of natural price equilibrium. Typically, it is better economically for the carrier to pay our lease rate than to make the capital investment to build its own tower and then the ongoing operating expense to maintain it for the carrier's own use. There is also a significant speed advantage for the carrier in collating on an existing tower. Since the carrier building its own tower is our typical competition, we compete with speed and with reasonable pricing, so that it is more sensible for the customer to lease space on our site.

Our competitiveness and technical knowledge is also bolstered by our executive and field management members, many of whom have prior work experience with our carrier customers. We also hire an external consulting firm that works with the carriers on technology strategy and engineering activities. Between those two sources, we stay abreast of technology developments with timely and high quality information. In addition, when we meet with our customers, we typically ask them about their technology plans directly as part of our normal dialogue.

Technology is important for American Tower because advancements in wireless technology often result in new network investments by our customers that then drive demand for more tower space. Our towers themselves don't have technology obsolescence risk. At the end of the day, we are essentially agnostic about the specific technology device of our customers, as long as they are advancing their networks to the next generation, in which, generally, additional equipment or frequencies on the tower, additional new sites or both are required.

Three Golden Rules for Success

To paraphrase one of our analysts, the first rule for success in the tower sector is to acquire assets at appropriate prices using a reasonable growth forecast to support that price. A tower asset has two main components of value, the existing customers that are on the site and the potential for new customers to be added. Overestimating the long-term financial value of the current customers or the number and timing of our new customers in the future can lead to overpricing a tower asset.

The second part of the conventional wisdom in the tower industry is that, if you are going to be the tower company, avoid branching off into business lines with lower margins, less operating leverage or high volatility.

The third rule is to manage your financial leverage because financial markets will fluctuate. You want to make sure that you have some breathing room in your financial plan, in case a recession or tightening of the capital markets occurs. Our company is moving toward leverage of four to six times net debt to ebitda, which we believe is a reasonable range for a business with high operating margins and long-term lease contracts.

Reducing Costs

With respect to our own telecom infrastructure costs, we have been successful in reducing our landline voice costs fairly dramatically. We've been able to take advantage of overcapacity and companies that have come out of restructuring for our long distance service. The service level risk on landline telephony is not that great because the networks are mature and generally reliable.

To control wireless telephony costs, I believe there are two ways to go about it. One is to try to have a master agreement for the entire company for all your wireless use, but if you've got people in different territories, the coverage and the quality of service may be inconsistent. Features may also be of differing value. Some parts of your company may need a direct-connect capability, and others may not.

I would suggest to other companies that they really understand what they need in each of their functions and territories. Decide if you want to try to aggregate nationally or if you want to continue to select service locally and then aggregate your business at the appropriate level and bid out your company to the quality carriers in the area. Once you come to that decision, if you have more than a few lines, you should be able to drive some price benefit and maybe even feature benefit, too. For instance, you could say, "If you want my business, then everybody gets free voice mail," or something along that line. It doesn't hurt to ask. There are five or six competitors out there, which is what the FCC wanted when it did the PCS auction, so customers could have choices.

The third aspect of telephony service, the data network, is mission-critical for most businesses. Therefore, you need a provider that has a reputation of standing behind its quality of service commitments, as well as offering a competitive price.

Finding New Customers

In the U.S., there are a couple of important attributes of a successful wireless company and its customer base. One is the net addition of customers to the company during a given period of time. A successful wireless company can be described as one that has a high share of industry net additions. In order to get that, you need to take two factors into account, which are the gross additions—new customers who just signed up or switched from another carrier—minus the ones that left (known as "churn"). For the new customers that sign up, what the successful wireless carrier needs to provide is network quality.

Perhaps the most important attribute of a successful wireless carrier is the quality of network that people experience at home, in the office or traveling, whether for business or pleasure. A solid wireless network begins with a "coverage footprint," which can be best described as the broad area where there is a usable signal. You then need to improve the signal capacity and strength within that footprint. The carriers that seem to be most successful in network quality are those that have had the steadiest capital expense budgets and commitment to network development over a long period of time.

The second attribute that draws brand new customers or switchers from other carriers is reputation developed through the advertising and marketing message. Consistency and investment in brand development and the ubiquity of the advertising message is key. The advertising message should be specific and emphasize either a great network or a low price.

A third driver of new additions is channel availability. Customers should be able to sign up for service in ways and locations that are convenient for them. Successful carriers develop a mix of owned, branded stores, kiosks, "stores within a store," resellers and direct sales force teams to reach out to prospective customers. A carrier's "channel landscape" is one of its most important strategies. This is especially the case in today's environment, where well known media and other brands are buying network capacity wholesale and competing in the retail market against the traditional carriers. A recent example is the announcement by ESPN that it will be launching its own branded wireless service.

Keeping New Customers

The best way to retain customers is through network quality. If a subscriber can't use his or her phone from the different locations that are important to him or her, the customer is going to try somebody else. The subscriber may not even know if there's anyone who's better but believe his or her current service is just not good enough, so he or she is going to switch.

Customer service is another tool to prevent churn. If a subscriber has a question on his or her bill and it gets resolved the first time by a courteous, knowledgeable rep, it helps to keep people on your system.

A third attribute that can keep your subscribers with you is a special feature, whether it is pricing or physical features of the service. Nextel has what almost everyone considers the best push-to-talk "walkie-talkie"-type service out there, and that keeps people on Nextel. Once people start using that feature and develop a circle of either friends or business associates that also use it, they tend not to leave that system easily.

For wireless carriers, keeping their subscribes on board continues to be tough, but the carriers are benefiting from the overall expansion of the wireless customer base. The whole wireless industry is growing, as more people are getting comfortable with wireless service and feeling like they have to have it. Using a wireless phone, or even a data device, is becoming a very typical part of the modern American lifestyle.

The Impact of Terrorism

One of our subsidiaries that we later sold had an office in the World Trade Center on September 11, which happened to be my second day as the president of the company. Unfortunately, we lost thirteen employees that day. It was devastating to our organization, but the company, our employees and our suppliers banded together to do our best to help the families. The economic effects of the attack, coupled with the recession that had already started before September 11, resulted in a severe period of dislocation in the telecom industry. Consequently, 2002 was a most difficult year for our company.

The threat of terrorism today does not affect our tower assets directly because we have 15,000 different locations. It is very unlikely that a terrorist event would affect very many of those assets. However, from a macroeconomic and business client view, we are very concerned about future terrorist attacks. The way we manage this and other business risks is that we scenario plan. In other words, we assign probabilities different possible outcomes. Then, we make decisions that will work out in an acceptable result in any of those scenarios. Let's assume 40 percent of the scenarios support our base case business plan, enabling us to meet our financial guidance. There may be a 30 percent case that you could do better than that because wireless subscriber growth is faster than expected and data comes in more quickly. Migration from pure landline phones to the wireless hybrid could also increase penetration faster than anticipated.

That leaves a potential downside scenario, which might be in the 20 to 30 percent range, that might occur if there's a terrorist attack, a recession or if the major wireless companies don't build as many new sites in their networks. We have our business plan worked out so that, if either the downside case or the upside case happens, we will not be damaged in the downside case, nor will we be unable to take advantage of the opportunity in the upside case. Our objective is to limit risk on both sides and never get into an unrecoverable position.

The Future of Customer Service

Competition to keep customers will be partly based on customer service and the responsiveness that people have to individual customers. If you are talking about business-to-business, which is what we are engaged in, customer service can benefit your growth rate, as long as you have enough assets in the right places. We believe we do, and we are focused on customer service on the sales side of our activities and in being fast, complete and accurate in the information we give our customers, enabling them to make a buying decision quickly and confidently. We execute thousands of leases a year so we have to create a consistent track record and continually demonstrate our proficiency.

Future Profit Areas

It is a long-term approach, but additional profit areas can be found for a telecom company that differentiates the kind of voice service it provides. The opportunity lies in both network quality and features perspectives. Making one wireless carrier's offering demonstrably better or different than the other five or six in a given marketplace is where there is an opportunity for price appreciation (higher rates for a clearly better or more interesting product). Demonstrably, higher quality features would also reduce churn, which remains the greatest opportunity for increasing profits in the wireless industry.

There is a huge cost to the switching of wireless customers. When most wireless customers end their relationship with their carrier, they just don't give up their cell phone; they go to another carrier. We calculated that churn cost the wireless industry more than $12 billion in 2003. Every time a customer switches, he or she typically gets a new handset, which is subsidized by the carrier. There's also advertising and employee selling cost in trying to replace the customers that a carrier has lost with new ones.

The profit opportunity for wireless phone companies is diverse. Network quality, especially in residential areas where it is weak right now, is an opportunity. Features like the Nextel's push-to-talk can make it more interesting for someone to have a wireless phone. The hybrid concept of wire-line in the house and wireless outside the house is another area that could drive penetration and attract more customers.

Wireless is an exciting industry that will experience sustained growth and will change the way we all communicate. Telephony services are moving inexorably toward greater mobility, and even the largest wire-line carriers are driving this trend. At American Tower, we're pleased to be an integral part of this industry. We are confident that our three-pronged strategy of smart growth, operational excellence and optimized financing will prolong and strengthen our success. It's an exciting road ahead, and the people throughout our company are eager to stay on the forefront of building a great foundation for the wireless future.

Jim Taiclet was named chief executive officer in October 2003 and chairman of the board in February 2004, succeeding Steve Dodge in both of these roles. He was appointed president and chief operating officer of American Tower Corporation in September 2001.

Mr. Taiclet also serves on the Board of Directors of FiberTower, which provides microwave-based backhaul services for wireless carriers and is a member of the FCC Media Security and Reliability Council. Mr. Taiclet joined American Tower from Honeywell International, where, as president of Honeywell Aerospace Services, he led a global organization of 10,000 employees, providing aircraft equipment repair, part distribution, logistics and space operations services.

Prior to Honeywell, Mr. Taiclet served as vice president, engine services at Pratt & Whitney, a unit of United Technologies Corporation. He was also previously a consultant at McKinsey & Company, specializing in telecommunications and aerospace. He began his career as an Air Force officer and pilot and served in the Gulf War.

Mr. Taiclet holds a Masters in Public Affairs from Princeton University, where he was a Wilson Fellow, and is a Distinguished Graduate of the United States Air Force Academy.

The Ever-Growing Wireless Industry

John Elms
President & CEO
SpectraLink Corporation

Introduction

The wireless industry is taking up a stronger and more integral role in daily lives across America. SpectraLink Corporation's wireless telephones are changing the way people communicate in the workplace. We strive to work within the wireless industry to provide freedom for employees that work in offices and whom otherwise probably use mobile voice devices on the road and at home. However, one of the misconceptions among the general public is that there is merely one wireless industry. The cellular telephone industry happens to be the most dominant segment, but, within the enterprise, we are seeing a growth of wireless local area networks (WLANs). These networks, which carry data, as well as voice, are opening a world of mobile opportunities for the workplace.

We at SpectraLink have principally focused on three key vertical markets; health care, retail and the manufacturing sector. Three to five years ago we were a small, steadily growing company, making our market in those key verticals. Because mobility very quickly turned into productivity for these key sectors, demonstrating a clear return on investment (ROI) was immediate and resulted in rapid market penetration for SpectraLink. Workplace mobility, however, extends beyond health care, retail and manufacturing. The fact is, mobility in the workplace provides enterprises across the board with productivity they long ago experienced in their personal lives.

Our key driver in the enterprise space is the fact that convenience and mobility are so prevalent in every other aspect of our lives. When we leave work, we use a cell phone; when we go home, we use a cordless phone. It doesn't make sense to most workers that they should be chained to their desks. It doesn't make sense to us, either, and we've provided the means to eliminate this final chain.

We've solved the issues that make cell phones not viable within the enterprise; durability, voice quality, call coverage within buildings and, most importantly, seamless integration with the enterprise telephone switch. Our products bridge that gap, bringing high quality mobile communications to the workplace.

However, we still have some issues to face within the industry. The biggest misconception is that WLANs are being fully deployed rapidly across *all* enterprises. While we look to the day that SpectraLink voice is just another application that is deployed on ubiquitous WLANs throughout the general enterprise market, that day has not arrived quite yet.

A key problem for us is that, as a player in the wireless industry, SpectraLink is often compared to consumer-targeted devices, such as cell phones and PDAs. The consumer devices turn over their products more quickly and have a much lower price point than enterprise devices based on orders of magnitude differences in volume. This disparity presents demands for comparable features but is typically overcome based on the value delivered.

Things are constantly changing around us. As we see this evolution of mobile voice and data becoming ubiquitous, standards have a critical role in getting us there. Standards have always preceded widespread adoption.

We can point to several technologies that are now mainstream as a result of emergence of standards. Take, for instance, the fax machine. When I first started my career, one user would have to configure the fax machine to respond to another user's to make sure the two fax machines would "talk" to one another. The CCITT Group 3 then established standards for faxes, and fax use became widespread across all businesses.

We also see a typical technology adoption curve, where you initially have a productivity tool that then becomes a convenience tool and then, finally, becomes ubiquitous. Laptops evolved in this way. Previously, only highly specialized individuals carried these portable computers because they had to conduct work offsite. Then, the general business community at large adopted the technology. Now, even my seventy-year-old father carries it with him to check e-mail when he travels.

SpectraLink is moving from a productivity tool to a convenience tool in the business sector. We are on the cusp of the second phase of the technology adoption curve.

Standards have taken on an extremely valuable role in the wireless industry because they precede widespread adoption.

Wireless in Our Everyday Lives

Today, it is practically impossible to get by in the business world, or even in a simple fast-paced society, without having access to, or using, wireless products. People have come to expect mobility in their everyday lives. We have cordless phones at home and cell phones in our pockets, but when we get to the office we are still typically "chained" to our desks. As consumers, we have justified the ROI of mobility by being able to multitask and increase our availability and responsiveness.

For businesses that deploy wireless communication, they experience similar and substantial improvements in customer service and responsiveness. For instance, in the health care market, equipping nurses with wireless telephones allows them to provide better, more responsive care for their patients. In retails stores, overhead paging is eliminated, creating a more comfortable and enjoyable shopping atmosphere for their customers. By unchaining key personnel from their desks, we're freeing and empowering their specific work-styles.

We make money by selling wireless telephone systems for the workplace that provide a value to the customers who purchase them. We provide value to our customers by delivering them with the means to make their high value people more productive. Our systems allow people to work the way they need to work, when they need to work, where they need to work and focus on enabling their work-styles for productivity and efficiency.

In SpectraLink's early life, we focused on delivering the best product for the best value. We focused on resources to develop it, manufacture it and market it. We are now in a product leadership position. As we've grown our business, we are moving toward a market-oriented position, spending more time with our customers and our investors to position us for the next phase.

In the wireless industry, we have seen a dynamic market that is ever-changing. We seek input from our teams that interface regularly with customers. We want to know what our customers want in a wireless product, how the needs of their workplaces are shifting. We also solicit feedback from our partners, from our resellers. It is an ongoing process.

The Inner Workings of a Wireless Company

I have been able to work with this company from a variety of different standpoints and have learned many things about business. I have been able to accomplish a lot. My position has given me operational experience, strong communication skills, made me open to new thoughts and ideas, and it's also given me the opportunity to complement my strengths with a very competent team.

Certainly, each company's CEO brings a unique background to the position. My own experience as VP of Operations has, probably, influenced my own style most significantly. In some ways, operations requires the broadest understanding of how the company works.

I know this company. I personally know all my team members and employees at all levels. I am intimately familiar with how the many facets of the company work together, and I am able to make sense of the many suggestions that we encourage our employees to provide.

The role I play is to provide leadership to the company, particularly within the industry segments in which we participate. The three main attributes of this role are to:

1. Be a visionary and communicate an understanding of what the future brings;
2. Set the course, direction and strategy for the company;
3. Establish a leadership tone of winning that resonates with the employee culture.

I work closely with the entire executive team, but I am keenly sensitive to engineering as a product leadership company.

Because I am not an engineer by training, I devote a lot of personal time in that area to round out my abilities. Today, I spent an hour with one of the senior software developers, receiving a tutorial, learning the intricacies of our radio design and its control, in order to deliver better-than-standard quality of service. I try to do that a lot. At forty-five, I'm not going to become an engineer, but I can stay close to my team and look to complement its technical skills with my insights into the market and its dynamics.

In addition, I consult regularly with the board, particularly the chairman. I find my board very supportive of the company's strategy, as well as of me personally. Our board represents the best possible combination of experience to provide me with advice and counsel based on their individual backgrounds. It is comprised of people who are experienced former CEOs, venture capitalists, public accounting partners and international executives. In short, they have been there, done that. As a bonus, some of them have a longstanding relationship with the company that gives them an invaluable perspective.

I work with my executives in partnership to realize the common goals of the company. They are the experts in their individual disciplines, and I treat them as such. I help them integrate their thoughts, plans and programs into a cohesive corporate plan that prioritizes the success of the company above the needs of the individual functions.

In doing this, I employ self-directed, energized leaders. I am able to set the tone for the company. I hold people accountable, and I foster a team environment that works collaboratively.

One of the biggest changes to occur in the company over the past year is the way in which our management team operates. Our former CEO and founder is a brilliant leader that tended to work with each of his executives one-on-one. Because we have a fairly new executive team, I have adopted a management team-oriented approach to running the business, so that all members of the team can benefit from the different experience sets we all bring to our roles.

Working with the Team

Our company is only as good as the people that we work with. We invest the most money in intellectual capital, the valued and talented people who work with us. There are specific traits we seek in prospective employees that increase their likelihood of success in this industry are the following:

- *Intelligence.* With an innate curiosity and desire to learn, employees funnel a constant flow of ideas. Our industry is a very challenging one that requires ongoing learning and a continuous grasp of new ideas;
- *Leadership skills.* Leadership skills, at any level of the company, turn employees into problem solvers. While management teams are in place to work with employees on a variety of issues that crop up on a daily basis, having employees with strong leadership skills across the company certainly makes our processes more efficient;
- *Team play.* No one person can do everything, and nothing can be more valuable than collaboration among a group of intelligent, competent people;
- *A track record of proven success.* We all build upon our previous experiences, and building a track record of success demonstrates initiative and accountability.

Opportunities for the company are constantly emerging, and you never want to let one slip by you. I sit down regularly with our teams to assess opportunities that we have in front of us, evaluating our ability to realistically capitalize on what could become valuable prospects.

While each executive has individual goals, our success as a company is the key driver in the goal setting process. Ultimately, the goals center on growing the market and the company's position within it, in order to maximize returns to our shareholders.

Success also means responding to difficulties and challenges head on, no matter what the scale of the situation. Particularly for CEOs, maintaining strong leadership, despite any company employment changes, is critical. In the first half of 2004, two of our four key executives opted to retire and leave the industry. During this period of transition, their individual management teams stepped up and collaborated with me to keep the business on track. One of the reasons we were successful in this transition period was by strongly involving the executive management teams in discussions and empowering them to make decisions, collaborate on plans and programs. We held people accountable, and they effectively stepped up to the plate, producing exemplary results.

Our team is the backbone of our company. We have an exceptionally talented development team that is innovative and quick to respond to changing technology shifts. In the event that a breakthrough technology would shift market dynamics as we know them, we would respond rapidly through technological innovation of our own. In addition, the product loyalty we have fostered in partners and customers would certainly play a role in our maintaining our product leadership position in the industry. If market competition were to skyrocket, we would work closely with our partners and customers to best understand the competitive threat, and we would leverage our relationships and sales force to aggressively target new competitors.

It is important to always keep our eye on what we are doing. My nightmare would be a loss of direction or focus. SpectraLink has remained profitable and has continued to grow based on a strict focus and aggressive development road map. We know good companies don't just happen. A successful company is always a work in progress, and we take very careful measures to ensure goals are met and that the entire company is on board with our vision.

We also are very aware of the changing competitive landscape. By conducting strong competitive and market intelligence, we are better prepared to best understand the direction and initiatives of our competitors.

Keeping up with the Pace

As I have mentioned, everything is always moving rapidly around us, and it is important to stay centered and stay at the top of our game. You've got to stay on top of the industry. The wireless world is ever changing, and the business of our customers is constantly growing and evolving. Reading periodicals and business books is a must, as is networking with other industry leaders. Through the years, these business relationships become invaluable. Learning is a two way street. In my position as a board member of the Mountain States Council of American Electronics Association, I've been able to share thoughts and ideas with government and industry leaders, while working to advance the electronics industry as a whole. People are a priceless resource, and nothing trumps the industry lessons we can exchange with our colleagues.

Spending time with my family also has proven to be an excellent venue for me to keep my edge. As CEO of a Nasdaq-listed company, my wife's ongoing support is invaluable, and my two teenage sons keep me busy. I take time to retreat to the mountains as often as I can to share time with my family. A breath of fresh air can do wonders for productivity.

Of course, everyone needs their own indulgences as well. Mine is continued study of Mandarin Chinese. I began learning the language while working in north Asia for several years, and I enjoy any opportunity to study the language further. Toward this end, I have an excellent tutor that tolerates nothing less than perfection.

I find that open communication with my key staff members that are engrossed in the industry, market and our partners is really the most effective resource I have. I am extremely lucky to have worked with CEOs that have brilliant leadership skills, albeit, they vary in style. The breadth of visionaries in the industry is amazing. Bruce Holland, SpectraLink founder and my predecessor as CEO, brought a tremendous focus to his position at a time of shifting market dynamics. Bruce always focused on a core set of values that served me well in operations, and that served the company extremely well in a broader sense. His time and his energy were based on ROI calculations; what is the return for this investment, and does it deliver value to customers? Bruce consistently counseled that a product company must be rigorous in the combined areas of cost and quality. These two attributes provide tremendous flexibility to respond to technical and competitive challenges that may be presented from time to time.

I also have great respect for my former CEO at PictureTel, Norman Gaut. During my tenure there, we doubled the company revenue for seven consecutive years, and, today, I still look to Norman for insight into managing growth, moving from niche to mainstream. It is through this relationship that I was able to recruit SpectraLink's first international board member, Werner Schmucking. Norman made the key suggestion of adding an international board member that could provide us with feedback and guidance into international markets. Norman was gracious enough to make a very valuable introduction, and his advice has proven invaluable, as we are now building the relationships in Europe that will support our growth objectives.

My time living and working in northern Asia also provided me with valuable lessons that I apply in my management style. In the several years I lived in northern Asia, I built a wide network of professional acquaintances. As divisional manager for PictureTel, I worked in Asian markets from an operational and general management standpoint. When you are working in a culture that is foreign to you, not only in language, but also in behavior, there are many lessons learned that certainly transpire into my current leadership role at SpectraLink.

I learned very early on in my time there that you don't necessarily need to emulate cultural behaviors but, rather, build respect for them. I have no doubt violated many behavioral rules unknowingly, but, with respect and kindness for your business partners, as well as your adversaries and competitors, people don't expect you to be something that you are not, so long as you are genuine.

Whether conducting business in Japan, Germany or in managing employees in Boulder, the key is to respect people. It's a basic and fundamental behavior, and it will open amazing doors.

Looking Ahead

As SpectraLink moves forward, there are many things to keep in mind. Over the last five to ten years, the business has become more mainstream, bringing an increase in standards and the potential for new competitors.

The Ever-Growing Wireless Industry

In two to five years, we will see the acceleration of standards, along with the convergence of voice and data, which will lead to increased competition in the industry.

For us, the major change is our move from a vertical market solution and application to a more mainstream communications product for the enterprise.

As different product types emerge for customers, we stand strong with our intimate understanding of customer needs.

If there were three "Golden Rules" for working in the wireless industry, they would be:

1. *Know your customer and market and be flexible enough to respond to their needs.* For instance, for the past decade, SpectraLink has only sold a black handset. By listening to our customers, we discovered that the health care market, in particular, had a need for a different colored handset more akin to the other technology products that they deploy.

2. *Deliver value.* We understand the purpose of what we ultimately deliver to our customers. We sell more than just a handset; it's a productivity device that empowers our customers' work-styles to better serve their customers.

3. *Dedicate yourself to standards.* In the world of Wi-Fi, we are reliant on our technology partners to provide the infrastructure for our handsets. We are enthusiastic participants in moving the whole industry forward and are absolutely committed to standards.

For someone looking to get involved in this business, there is much to know and much to be gained. I have found some important sources of this information in local books. I would first advise that any book that is published on our industry is, most probably, out of date the minute it hits the shelves. That being said, three books that I would recommend to anyone in the business world are Jim Collins' *Good to Great*, *The Discipline of Market Leaders* by Treacy and Wiersema and *The Art of War* by Sun Tzu.

I intend to keep SpectraLink in the prosperous position it is in, while allowing it to expand in the future. There are steps that I take in my business life to accomplish these things. I personally visit top customers and partners to stay abreast of market trends and customer issues. The greatest difficulty faced is identifying the differences between seemingly "good ideas" and viable future products and in ensuring that receiving information is not construed as a commitment to re-architect a particular solution to fit a point product need. In doing this, we are working toward being responsive to our customers, and, in doing so, we stay close to our markets, so as not to miss a shift in customer sentiment or market demand.

I test and use our products on an ongoing basis to ensure that they meet the standard of product leadership. I use our wireless telephones both in the workplace and at home. My VPs of engineering and operations are involved in the feedback and learning process. It is only through the use of the products as a customer that we can truly appreciate customers' experiences and continuously improve our products.

I have a breadth of international experience working in a global marketplace, and, therefore, I personally guide our international expansion strategy. With international sales at 5 percent of total company revenue in our most recent quarter, this is our greatest opportunity to accelerate the growth of the company as a whole. The vice president of international operations is a close collaborator in this endeavor. Our success will be to offer international customers what long-standing competing technologies have not been able to do, and that is to offer an effective voice solution that interoperates with an enterprise's overall communication strategy.

In conclusion, it is important to know your audience and learn how to communicate your ideas effectively. The most brilliant innovations will die a slow death if the originator fails to enlist support for them from the people necessary for adoption.

And finally, don't be afraid to ask for advice. If you are willing to learn, you can be taught.

John Elms is the president and CEO for SpectraLink Corporation. Prior to taking on the company's leadership position, Mr. Elms became intimately familiar with all facets of the company as vice president of operations, which included overseeing manufacturing, distribution and worldwide customer services.

Mr. Elms built his extensive experience in the tech sector, domestically and internationally, at the cusp of VIP's explosion in the market. Mr. Elms worked with PictureTel Corporation in various sales and service capacities, most recently as the vice president of Americas service and corporate support. Mr. Elms was also the director of Asia-Pacific and Japan, operating out of Hong Kong, for the enterprise services division of PictureTel, responsible for business development and service delivery throughout the Asia-Pacific region.

Mr. Elms holds a Bachelor of Liberal Arts degree from Harvard University.

Developing High-Value Solutions for Wireless Carriers

Jim Grady
Vice President, Worldwide Sales
Ditech Communications

The Wireless Industry

The wireless industry continues to be characterized by rapid growth, in both the technologies and the services sold to the end users. That pace is not slowing; if anything, it's accelerating. Ditech Communications is a medium-sized supplier of network infrastructure equipment for wireless carriers. To be successful within this segment, companies need to focus on an area where they can deliver high value solutions and outperform their competitors, specifically, by creating applications (made up of products & service) that help the wireless carriers achieve their goals to grow revenue or reduce cost.

Our Company

Ditech Communications develops, manufactures and sells core network infrastructure equipment for telecommunications service providers, specifically, voice processing equipment used to enhance the voice quality of a phone call. Ditech is the only company in the voice processing space that has continued to invest heavily in new product development. Other companies in this space seem to have invested in segments viewed as more attractive, treating voice processing as a cash cow.

Ditech, instead, has gone deeper into the segment we serve, allowing us to innovate and create new, higher value-added applications that provide new growth opportunities, while increasing our market share in traditional applications. Investment in entering a number of high opportunity international markets is a third avenue for continued growth at Ditech.

The Right Product Mix

Selecting the right product mix has a creative/expansive portion and an analytical portion. The creative/expansive part is driven, first, by our customers and, second, by our capabilities and technology.

By staying very close to our customers, we can recognize opportunities to help them achieve their business goals and address emerging challenges in their networks. When we see an opportunity, we work with customers to refine the idea into a possible product or solution.

Developing High-Value Solutions for Wireless Carriers

In addition, Ditech looks at its capabilities to see where these can be leveraged into new growth. Can our sales channel sell another related product to the existing target cellular carrier? Can we develop other related products with the proprietary technology we have developed?

During the analysis phase, we will evaluate each new product opportunity against each other. The criterion is total market size and our likelihood of success. The competitive landscape and how closely the new product matches our capabilities are some of the factors that allow us to assess our prospects.

Once in the implementation phase, we invest in platforms that can ultimately become a number of different products over time. Platforms have a longer product lifecycle than individual point products.

In a company like Ditech, research and development is the biggest expense. These development costs don't stop once a product reaches the market. There is a cycle of investment in an individual product that is high at the start and tapers off over time. R&D development is ongoing due to the regular stream of new products demanding investment.

Staying Ahead of the Technology Curve

We focus on our core strength, which is integrating leading technology components and subsystems and developing high-reliability, highly scalable systems. We use the very latest chips, chassis and other components, and we integrate them and develop the operating system software to make it a solution. This gives us leading edge technology without and limits our exposure to "bleeding" edge technology.

Customer Service the Right Way

Telecom carriers really don't buy products; they only buy solutions. The solution includes all aspects of deploying the product in order to operate it in the network, and a company expects it to be in its network for five or seven years. Therefore, customer service is a critical element of selling the solution. If the customer does not perceive your company to have that ability, you won't even get the first meeting.

55

To stay close to the customer base, we talk to customers a lot. For me, personally, and for the entire executive team, we have to be at the customer location, in the field, fairly regularly. Some companies leave direct customer contact to the sales team and expect reports back to headquarters. We think that is a big mistake, as valuable information about the marketplace, the technology and the customer gets filtered out in the communication process.

For example, the VP of engineering and I recently went to China together to spend a week talking to customers and partners there. Getting the VP of engineering out in the field allows him to be that much closer to what's going on, so he is aware of the challenges and problems that occur with our customers.

The number of wireless carriers in the world is relatively limited. Therefore, I have met with all of our biggest customers, as well as all the most promising prospects, personally. This does require me to do loops around the globe quite often, but it's necessary to have that relationship with the sales team, so that you can understand the sales team's challenges, how we're executing and how the customer perceives us.

The Changing Industry

There have been several big changes in the industry over the last five to ten years. In the late 1990s, we went through the telecom bubble, the bust and then the nuclear winter that followed and wiped out a ton of small startup companies. At the same time, the pace of technology has continued to evolve quickly.

Shorter product life cycles have had a big impact on the equipment infrastructure business. In the past, once a carrier for deployment selected you, you could deploy for years and years. However, that's no longer true. New products follow more quickly, and your product can become uncompetitive very quickly if you don't continue to develop it and make newer, denser, more capable solutions.

Separately, international markets have become much more important. In the past, a U.S. equipment company would sell in the domestic market for some time before even considering going internationally with a product. Now, sometimes, the first markets you sell to are international because that's where they're buying the products. For example, with DSL, some of the first heavy deployments were in Asia, not in the U.S.

The cost side of the telecom equipment business has also changed. More and more companies have moved parts of their developments offshore to lower costs and to get the benefit of round the clock development. The rise of the contract manufacturer has allowed equipment suppliers to focus their energy and capital on the high value added R&D, instead of manufacturing.

Over the next five to ten years, it's going to get more competitive. For example, in developed countries, the growth in the end customer markets for cellular is slowing and we are seeing consolidation. The mergers in the U.S. include (i) Cingular and AT&T and (ii) Nextel and Sprint. As our carrier customers face greater cost pressure, it will ultimately mean more competition for suppliers.

While the growth is already leveling off in developed markets, there is still a ton of growth in less developed markets, so that's where we have begun investing. The biggest markets for cellular are now China and India.

Selling Globally

Creating a Strategy

To create a strategy for selling globally, we start with a review of the size and timing of the market (countries/regions). When will a marked deploy a technology? It's good to go to a leading market for early learning about customers' needs and gain early deployment experience. For example, if you were selling GSM in the mid-'90s, then all the early customers were outside the U.S. If you waited until a U.S. carrier was interested in GSM, your products would be a generation behind those of your competitors that sold and deployed GSM in Europe.

Market size also matters; sometimes a few large international markets are bigger than the U.S. market.

Do not view the world as U.S. and International; justify the investment for each region or a country. You can't be successful unless you make an investment into a market. You need to understand what your costs are going to be, as well as your distribution strategy to go out and invest in a market. You make the investment decisions, market-by-market.

Differences in Selling Globally

Obviously, the distribution is done very differently internationally. Most companies sell direct in the U.S. Internationally, until your company is fairly large, you don't sell direct; you sell through VAR (Value-Added Reseller) and agents in most all cases. However, what people don't realize is that you still need to have a direct relationship with your customer.

You can't expect the VAR and the agent to just take care of everything. You really still need to be there. Some people think, "I don't need a single person. I'll just have a VAR or an agent, and they'll take care of it," but that's just not realistic. You have to be aware of the many pitfalls of not understanding what's going on. Local knowledge is very important.

Global Challenges

The challenges internationally vary by market. There are credit issues everywhere; there are distribution issues everywhere. There are countries where, legally, your distributor becomes exclusive if you enter a contract with him or her. You have to watch out for that, as it can prevent your company from having the right number and type of partners you need to be successful.

There are legal issues about permanent entity establishment. If you even go sell in a country, you may be establishing a permanent entity (according to the laws in a specific country), and then you start getting taxed. There are also regulatory issues. Sometimes, there is taxation based on hardware versus software, which is defined differently in each of the countries that do that.

You need to have local knowledge. You can't do this without people locally who know how to do what you're doing. You can't carefully evaluate a market and qualify the customer prospects without knowing a lot about the market, the specifics and how to do business there.

Cultural Issues

It is important to have an understanding of the business culture where you plan on doing business. For example, Korea is, in some ways, similar to the U.S. in the discussions between a supplier and a customer. When a Korean customer asks, "When is the new product or feature available?" an appropriate response is to talk about a target date. The expectation is that you'll be pretty close to that date, and you'll keep them informed of any changes as you get closer to the date.

In Japan, the customer expects the response to represent a solemn commitment to the final delivery date. So, in Japan, you must be very conservative about the dates you discuss with a customer, or you jeopardize your credibility and, in the long term, your standing in the market.

When to Pursue Overseas Clients

If there are high fixed costs in your products, like a large R&D investment, it may be necessary to address a large market to stay cost competitive. You leverage your investment with incremental revenue at a much lower incremental cost. This is the typical situation in the telecommunications equipment business, where the cost to develop a new product is very high, but international standards ensure that a product will interoperate in a large number of countries.

In the cellular industry, there are several large companies that have operations in many countries. So, your customers may lead you into new markets to support their subsidiaries.

It is also important to understand the different markets. One country may be an early adopter of new technology and present opportunities for early learning and early revenue in a new product. Or you may find that there is larger revenue potential for your product in certain international markets.

Negotiating Tips

Start by understanding all the costs associated with the deal you are negotiating, everything from currency and bad debt risks to support cost, shipping, insurance and import taxes, if they apply.

Additionally, you need to put local people there and consider that along with the size of the deal, as well as the strategic issues. Does this get me entry into this region?

The question is whether you're selling to the end user or you're selling to a bar. Everything is easier if you're selling to a bar because, then, the bar takes on the negotiation with the end customer, and they have those relationships. In the U.S., you usually sell to a bar, so it de-risks you from the end transaction.

Homeland Politics

There is a certain level of frustration with the U.S. policy at this point. Now, there is certainly a distrust of America's policies everywhere around the world, and that's definitely a barrier. For instance, in certain countries, they really are actively trying to avoid buying U.S. products if they can.

On the other hand, if you have a product that makes sense economically for them, they will consider it. There are a couple of places that we can't sell in, such as enemy nations of the U.S., but, short of that, in most countries, you have a shot if you're not significantly disadvantaged.

Benchmarking Sales

Sales on an international basis are not benchmarked differently, per se, than they are measured domestically, but you do need to look at how long it has been since you entered a market. It takes some time to get up to speed, so you can't expect that, if you enter a market, six months later you'll have the maturity and sales revenue growth that you would see in a market you've been in for five years. The benchmarks have to consider how long you've been there and your level of investment in the country.

Structuring Your Overseas Investment

It is best to look at investing in developing sales in a new country or region as a long-term investment, realizing that you're going to spend money for, perhaps, a year before you're going to see the results really begin. You need to do your homework up front about the attractiveness of a market and all the costs that you expect to have. Make a plan of how much it will cost and for how long before you expect results. Then, you need to commit the resources and stay the course.

Jim Grady came to Ditech from Tenor Networks, where, residing in Shanghai, China, he was vice president of business development. Prior to Tenor, he spent three and a half years at TollBridge Technologies, a venture-backed manufacturer of VoIP access gateways where he was vice president of worldwide sales. In this position, he built successful OEM relationships and sales teams in the U.S., Asia and Europe. Mr. Grady previously held other senior level positions at TollBridge. From 1991 to 1999, Mr. Grady held a range of senior management positions in general management, sales and marketing for AirTouch Communications, Inc., (formerly PacTel Corporation and now Verizon Wireless/Vodafone), including market vice president and general manager and regional vice president and general manager. Prior to AirTouch, he was a consultant at the Boston Consulting Group. He holds a B.S. from the University of Maine in Mechanical Engineering and received his Masters of Business Administration from Harvard University.

Wireless Sales Strategies

Michael Z. Jones
Senior Vice President, Sales
STSN, Inc.

Introduction

The complexity of the initial HSIA sale is due to the conflict between the financial objectives of the manager, owner and franchisor. The property manger wants full properties and happy guests. Making guests happy requires investments to ensure that property meets the guests' expectations. The franchisor is focused on upholding the brand and, like the manager, is insistent on the property being representative of the brand. Worn carpet and dated décor are not desired by guests or tolerated by franchisors. And, finally, the owner and asset manager really only care about profit and return on investment.

Based on the ultimate purchasing decision being the responsibility of the owner's asset manager, and the goals associated with that role, there is the tendency of that decision to be based primarily on price, rather than value. This trend in the market allowed for many low cost integrators to enter the market, providing solutions that met the bare minimum of the properties' needs, simple Internet connectivity. The true service features and requirements (such as security, application support, etc.) to support the needs of the business traveler were often overlooked. In many cases, hoteliers have even gone to the extent of posting numerous "users beware" messaging in the guest rooms, noting that they are not responsible for the quality and safety of the HSIA services. A good way to keep costs low, but what impact has that had on guests?

As we look to the near future, we have noted this disconnect in the market and anticipate a shift in emphasis back to hotelier quality and accountability. Providing HSIA will no longer be the only requirement; rather, a quality service with quality support will be demanded by guests. Guests' dissatisfaction with quickly installed low cost systems will force owners to revisit their investments and augment current systems or replace them with higher quality solutions.

The Right Product Mix

A company should create product strategies based on an understanding of the markets it aims to serve and trends within those markets. It's a very predictable pattern. First, there's an event or an innovation based on the need of the market, and opportunistic providers rush to meet those needs with a new solution or offering. The greater the barriers of entry are to that market, and the more unique provisioning, the greater the opportunity of long-term success.

Following a market "needs requirements gathering" and "product definition," there is an initial launch of the product. Once the product is able to recover the cost of the product's creation and launch, this phase of sales results in the highest margins. The next phase of product evolution involves making the delivery of the product or service more scalable, through engineering more cost-effectively or being able to purchase and deliver more effectively in quantity. Elasticity of profit now becomes a driving characteristic of successful companies. Prices lower slightly, and margins aren't quite as strong, but significantly more revenue is being generated, and significantly increased profits are possible. This is typically the period of most rapid growth for a company.

Finally, there is a phase of product maturity. What you offered has now been well validated by the market. Competitors are going to copy what you do and sell it to the market that has been defined. Usually, the compelling value that they will try to use is to differentiate themselves by providing a lower price. If mass production is not a core competency, you should be well down the path to the next great product, because the end of life is near on the current offering.

The most recent example of an accelerated product life cycle that would be familiar to consumers is that of the Apple iPod. Released in the winter of 2001, this quirky music player was a shock to the consumer electronics industry. Previous MP3 players had a capacity of less that 64MB, or about twenty songs. The iPod suddenly provided eighty times the capacity with a 5mb player, and users had room for 1,500 songs. During 2002, Apple defined the MP3 player industry, shipping the iPod in quantity. From 2003 to the middle of 2004, Apple dominated the segment. Competitors were not yet able to offer a compelling enough products to overcome the momentum of the iPod. The product began to enter a mature phase at the end of 2004, as competitors were able to provide compelling price/value propositions and features to rival the iPod's strengths. While Apple continues to maintain a nice lead in the market at the end of 2004, it is forecasted that mass producers of consumer electronics will overtake that position in 2005.

In the case of STSN, we are the dominant shareholder of the market for HSIA services in a rapidly maturing hospitality industry. Our focus is on maintaining and expanding profitable market share with high value products and services. We face constant attempts by our competitors to commoditize the services we provide, delivering a cheaper but lower quality service to the market. Unless we are able to continue to understand and deliver the "high value" products needed in the market and deliver those products, we look forward only to escalating commoditization and pricing wars.

Expensive Ingredients

In the concession/revenue model previously discussed, the price that the provider pays to be in the real estate called a hotel is the most expensive element of cost of the service. Traditionally, the hotelier takes 50 percent of the gross revenues. The service provider is allotted the remaining 50 percent as of net revenue and provides all of the operating infrastructure and support services. All of the costs associated with providing that service is, then, the responsibility of the provider. In this business model, there is a natural tendency to focus on maximization of revenue and less emphasis on cost management.

In a managed services model, the provider provides the services on a "margin plus" product and services pricing model. Now, the provider's opportunity to generate a profit is tied directly to its ability to manage their its expenses. Every area of our company is deeply involved in the process of business re-engineering, as STSN shifts from a traditionally concession-based model to a managed services business.

Staying Ahead of the Curve

Staying ahead of the curve requires any company to stay in touch with the markets it serves. Unless you understand the needs of those markets, the technology or innovation you develop runs the risk of becoming irrelevant more quickly than you anticipate. Once the needs are understood, providing a differentiated solution to that need is critical. Despite the temptation, we have worked very hard to avoid engineering for engineering's sake. We've worked hard not to build "cool stuff" that might not meet the needs of the market. We would much rather have really boring, good product offerings that meet the needs of our industry.

An example of this may be seen in the genesis of STSN. The original services model was to automate the "hotel room of the future." In this "Jetson"-like concept, everything from personalized TV, radio, temperature controls and in-room menu was to be built on an application platform, utilizing a connection to the Internet. Upon closer review, it was determined that STSN could realize more immediate success by focusing on the need for HSIA services in the guest room.

A Successful Product

For a product concept to be considered as an opportunity at STSN, it would require a rapid adoption rate and revenue growth model. We would expect at least a 200 to 1,000 percent growth rate in year-over-year revenues in the second year of sales. In terms of profitability of the product line, including all of the development, launch and management, we would expect to be fully profitable within eight months of product launch. We consider the life of any product to be from eighteen to thirty-six months. This culture is a function of being a technology driven company, where mass production and delivery are not the distinguishing competencies. By definition, we've got to achieve a very unrealistic metric of success and return on investment capital. We ensure that success by, first, doing our homework (the product marketing noted above) and, then, making every effort to flawlessly launch the product.

Effective Customer Service

STSN is in the hospitality business, and, in that business, service is core to the culture. From the Courtyard or LaQuinta to the finest Ritz hotel, the theme is the same; customer satisfaction. In some cases, a more cost-effective or value-driven version of that model might be in place (even to avoid dissatisfaction), but it is a part of every brand's mission statement and goals. STSN is, in effect, an extension of that brand and promise to the guest.

Customer service, above and beyond what is typically delivered by the telecommunications industry, is a required core competency for us as a provider in the hospitality market. For example, what happened the last time you tried to call your residential phone service or long distance provider, or your bank, or a consumer electronics company, or a computer manufacturer? Guests expect to be pampered when they stay in a hotel. Everything has to work, and if, for whatever reason, it does not work, you have to be ready to be there when the guest wants you. That availability must be at the guest's time and on his or her terms. Getting back to somebody between noon and three tomorrow, after they placed a call this evening, is not tolerated. You have to provide the answer and the solution to the customer on the phone, first call, within minutes, despite how challenging the set up or viruses on their computer might be.

There are several categories of customers in STSN's HSIA delivery model. One category would be the consumer in the guest room. We have surveyed our performance with those customers every day and gather the requirements and enhancement requests directly from our consumers. We have collected over 100,000 responses to our survey in 2004.

Another important customer in the STSN business model is the conference and event planner. In conjunction with the hotel's sales team, STSN provides pre-event requirements services. This allows us to sit down with the customer (the meeting planner) to understand his or her HSIA needs in the rooms and events area. We are then able to deliver a tailored solution to those conference HSIA requirements. STSN is also on-site during major events to react to any new needs or technical issues. Following the event, STSN performs a post-event debriefing and feedback session with the event planner. This allows us to have a first hand assessment on the effectiveness of our services and better understand future customer requirements.

We have many customers with differing types of needs, but we also have many different types of constituents. One example would be what many sales and marketing theorists would call the "distribution partner." We call it a "hotel." The hotel is the actual property and brand flag of the property. We work very closely to align our goals and activities to cooperatively meet the objects of STSN and the hotel. Strategically coordinating sales and marketing efforts allows us to fully maximize tour ability to provide for the hotels' guests needs. We have daily interaction on property and regular feedback and assessment sessions with brand flags quarterly. Formal assessment and scorecard efforts are conducted in-person.

Out of 2,400 properties in the U.S. with Marriott's brand name on it—Ritz Carlton, JW Marriott, Marriott, Renaissance, Residence Inn, Courtyard, Townplace Suites and Springhill Suites—Marriott Corporation only owns eleven of the total properties. Like Hilton, Starwood and IHG, Marriott is primarily a brand and franchise specialist and property management company. Real estate investment trusts and hospitality investment groups own the majority of hotels.

If somebody is deciding whether to make a decision to invest $250,000 to put a high-speed Internet access infrastructure into his or her property, the property owner is the financial holder of that decision. We work very closely with the owners to ensure that we are meeting their needs and planning for future portfolio requirements. As with the properties and brand flags, quarterly in-person assessments are performed. It's a very complex business model. To manage that, STSN has three primary sales divisions. The first is charted to work with the owners. This group has very strategic sales skills, as well as good quantification and financial backgrounds. The second sales organization is responsible for the sales activities on-property. They work with the property to ensure that the guest and meeting planers requirements are understood and fully delivered. The final group is targeted at the actual customer, the meeting and event planner. By orchestrating all elements of the industry, we are able to fully deploy services and maximize revenues.

Making It Happen

A key area of focus for all cross-functional organizations within STSN is "doing your homework." This is first seen in the requirements gathering and planning process. The goal is to understand what you are going to do before you burn any energy doing it. You have to have a market requirements document process. "Winging it" with products rarely (if ever) works. Again, in the homework section, if you're going to do a major project, you better have a very well-prepared scope of work, where you and your customer agree on what you're doing, how much you are charging and when the work is to be performed, so that neither of you are disappointed. Understanding and documenting the project requirements and properly setting expectations on the delivery of the project ensures payment upon completion and/or understanding if things go wrong.

The second area would be in process and execution. We have a very focused culture around process management. We practice elements of the Six Sigma methodology and other process re-engineering concepts. It's a process enhancement and development methodology that grew out of GE and Allied Signal. By understanding what has happened, learning form that example and applying what we learn to process improvement, we are able to learn from our mistakes, rather than repeat them unnecessarily.

While planning and process are important, nothing is more essential than effective communication. STSN performs very complex integrations of telecommunications environments involving many internal and external constituents. There might be a combination of an ownership group, the property development company, the brand flag and the on-property management company. In any one integration, there might be as many as four "bosses" or constituents that we have to interact with daily. Unless communication is flawless, trouble is just around the corner. Regular engagements, via conference call or in person, allow us to update and document progress and issues with all constituents. Formal agenda, minutes, action items capture and publication of note to all participants is a part of our culture that ensures effective communication.

By making core processes an intra-company competency, we are able to avoid many of the time sinks that affect most companies. While this enables us to be more effective, it also makes for a much more conducive work environment.

Emphasizing Success in Wireless Sales

Goals of My Position

In my role of senior vice president of sales, I am tasked with establishing channels of distribution that match the needs of our industry. It is a cornerstone of our culture that "we obtain unrealistic revenue goals every quarter." Our revenue growth has averaged 75 percent each year over the last two years. There are four areas of emphasis that make this lofty pattern of success possible.

First, 20 percent of my time is spent recruiting and networking with potential candidates. Hiring individuals with the skills and experience required is extremely difficult and time consuming, but hiring the right people has exponential results. Even when open positions are not available, there is a great deal of energy spent building a pipeline of versatile candidates. This allows for extremely quick recruiting and hiring when those positions are required.

Second, regular assessment and training of the team members allows for rapid growth. It is a great advantage to build a team of individuals that have diverse skills. Team members are measured and assessed relative to their qualitative, quantitative and communication skills. They have to adapt to changes very quickly. By providing them with the training to address opportunities for growth, they also have to be able to assume responsibility faster than should be expected.

The next area of focus is to ensure that each area of the sales organization has the tools necessary for success. You can have the greatest salespeople in the world, but they are not fully effective if they do not have what they need to do their jobs. Proper computing (including computer, customer relationship management system and remote Internet connectivity) and telecommunications tools are critical to effective sales efforts.

Finally, it is critical that the sales efforts be complemented and fueled by promotions and marketing efforts. The most critical dependency that the sales organization has within any company is with the marketing team.

Another 25 percent of my time is spent in strategic planning and reviews with the marketing team.

Extracting the Best Price

There are many issues to consider in evaluating how to maximize your average sales price. The first rule of thumb is to avoid the bad deals. There are the cases in every sales manager's experience when he or she is approached by a sales representative and briefed on a "strategic deal" that he or she has uncovered. A close examination of this opportunity results in an understanding of unrealistic customer expectations or unrealistic market pressures. Despite that understanding, there is a natural tendency to do everything possible to "win" the deal and not "loose" to a competitor. There are some cases where the worst thing that can happen is to "win" a bad deal. Over commitment to unprofitable terms should be opportunities given to a competitor.

Do everything you can to avoid deals that are based solely on price. Deals that extract a good price are deals that deliver value to the customer and are fair and equitable for both sides. Let me give you an example illustrating this by using "quality of service" as a means of differentiating a product offering:

In 2002, La Quinta hotels issued an RFP to the market for HSIA services to be integrated and supported into eighty properties in the US. La Quinta initially opted for a low cost provider based on being able to get the lowest price possible for installation and services. Shortly after the provider had installed ten properties, La Quinta realized the provider was not able to deliver the quality of services required. A second RFP phase was sent to five providers for a new solution.

STSN responded to that proposal with a solution that had the highest upfront investment required, as well as ongoing support costs that were higher in comparison to all other respondents. Instead of focusing on the price, the emphasis of the sales was on the value delivered in that price and the relative gains through "total value" and contribution to the La Quinta strategy. When La Quinta understood STSN's services and how those services supported their goals to change their brand image (the joke in the hospitality industry is that "La Quinta" loosely translated means next to Denny's), they chose the STSN solution. La Quinta wanted to be able to compete against Courtyard and be seen as a quality place to stay based on high value. As a result, STSN was able to charge 20 percent more than the other competitors and has been installed in eighty US properties. STSN is also slated to install and additional 285 La Quinta properties in 2005.

Empowering the Sales Team

The first principle of empowerment is to hire the right people with skills to assume responsibility and to have the ability to execute that responsibility effectively. It is the responsibility of the leadership to provide them with the vision and strategic direction, including the campaigns and efforts to push your products to markets and then get out of the way. It is critical that the sales organization has the ability and responsibility to move forward without unnecessary oversight. With that said, it is critical that leadership is accessible if needed. Give the guidelines and then measure sale organization's compliance to the guidelines, usually through compensation.

For example, one of our organizations is a strategic sales group selling very high priced ($50K-$1,000K) opportunities. These people are MBA-carrying sales representatives who have very good quantitative skills. They are given a set of guidelines and parameters that support our strategy (pricing, discount, promotions, etc.). They are able to maximize their compensations based on how they use these guidelines in support of company objectives.

Increasing Revenues/Reducing Expenses

STSN has increased revenues 75 percent per year for the past two years. If it was determined that success required increased growth rates, we would be required to enter more experimental market opportunities, consciously assuming the increased risk and potential increase in cost of sales that would affect profitability. By strategically focusing on specific areas of the market, we are able to maximize our efforts and continue to increase profitability. An example of this has been that STSN has continued to focus on the needs of properties that value high-quality services in the hospitality sector. Some competitors have chosen to move "down scale," attempting to sell to properties that are extremely price sensitive. By focusing on a smaller number of better opportunities, we have continued to have great success.

In a position where expenses must be reduced by 25 percent over the next year, it would be critical to understand the motivation behind the expense cuts. You would do something very different for a short-term or mid-term business cycle interruption versus a long-term change in the business.

For STSN, the weather in Florida was a difficult challenge in 2004. Many hotels were affected by the four hurricanes that hit Florida within one month. This short-term impact on business required us to tighten our belts but did not have an impact on headcount or long-term investments. Companies faced with long-term issues would do something very different. Facing a commoditized value proposition or an unanticipated competitive issue, companies are sometimes forced to restructure or radically shift strategy, affecting how expenses are allocated.

In everything we do, there are inefficiencies. Whether it's parking in short-term instead of long-term, ineffective meetings or ineffective use of time, there's always fluff. That goes for expenses as well. I think that expense management is something that, cyclically, is scrutinized and then forgotten. With the right planning and execution, operating expenses could be dropped by 25 percent over the short term, with limited impact on headcount. To sustain that rate over a longer period of time would eventually require a reduction in headcount.

Losing a Key Employee

If you're not occasionally losing key employees, one of two things is happening. Either you're not asking enough of them or not expecting them to grow quickly (if you're pushing people hard enough, at some point, they are no longer able to meet the challenge, and then they are limited to a specific role level or forced to do something else), or you don't have people who are good enough to be stolen by somebody else.

You have to plan in advance to lose key employees by grooming others for advancement. The only way to protect the organization and the company is to have an active pipeline of good candidates with a diverse skill set. Positions may not "be open," but always interview candidates and maintain a pipeline.

Increasing Output

If the budget were increased by 25 percent, the first area of investment would be in market share acquisition. Strike while the iron is hot, and acquire captive markets for distribution. As a result of this strategy, the first area of investment would be in sales and marketing. Being the sales guy, you should probably expect me to say that.

The success of those efforts would create activities in other areas. It would be reasonable to anticipate the increased demand on operations as a result of my success in sales. Effective execution and support of new business is critical for the maximization of revenue and profits.

The final area of investment focus would be to reinvest in marketing, building the product to address the future needs of the market. The remaining allocation of funds would go into product marketing and engineering.

Worst-Case Scenarios

The worst-case scenario, from a competitive standpoint, would be an attack to the market by a competitor with unlimited resources, who decides that the space we currently occupy is one they want. To address this threat, it would be wise to make every effort to ensure that the competitor understands that acquiring the company occupying the space they desire is the shortest route to their goal. In that event, the incumbent would get something other than a slow death.

From a partner standpoint, the worst-case scenario would be a partner that decides to take his or her relationship and knowledge to a competitor. The fact is that a good partnership would never fall into that trap. That scenario would be like being told by your wife that she wants a divorce and you're surprised. If that's the case, someone messed up a long time ago. Having direct and regular communication of objectives, strategy, execution and metrics is the core of a good partnership. Having that core would prevent that worst-case scenario from happening.

The worst thing that could happen to any company or team would be the unexpected departure, for any reason, of multiple leaders at any level. For example, if two or three members of the executive team or department leadership within a functional area left at the same time, the results would be catastrophic. An organization can weather the departure of any one, or maybe even two contributors, at an operational level. Losing more than two not only affects the orphaned organization, but, as other leaders attempt to fill that void, they are not able to effectively meet the needs of their primary areas of responsibility.

These organizational catastrophes are usually the result of one of three issues. First, there is the possibility of an accident or unforeseen event affecting the lives of more than one of those leaders at a given time. The second example would be a mass exodus of leadership due to discontent or active recruiting by another company. Finally, there is the chance of being caught in a case of bad timing. In looking at these possible causes, nothing can be done to prevent the first case, other than not allowing leadership to spend time together or travel together. In the second case, the situation can be prevented or influenced by the success or challenges within an organization. Once the commitment is made by leadership to leave, it is very difficult to persuade them to stay. Proper planning in organizational management can typically prevent the final case.

Sales Advice

Act fast; any opportunity may be gone tomorrow. In the world of technology and communications, the reality of Moore's Law makes that principle even more important. Everything has to be twice as fast or twice as big or half as much in price every eighteen months. Within any given product progression, wireless, for example, it has to improve that fast. Today's WiFi strategy may be made obsolete by WiMAX tomorrow. You have to execute very quickly on the products you have in hand today. Then you have to execute very quickly to understand what the products of tomorrow need to be.

In rapidly evolving markets, you don't have the luxury of somebody selling a product over a consistent period of time because the market and the technology that drives the solutions in the market change so rapidly. There have been many examples of "done deals" derailed due to technological advancement that makes the deal obsolete before the contracts could be completed. You have to act fast.

You have to listen. Typically, sales people have a tendency to want to be seen as the "expert," so they talk too much. If you're talking, the person you're interacting with can't tell you what you need to hear. If you're talking, you are unable to hear the customer trying to communicate his or her needs. Until you really understand the customer's needs, you can't give him or her the right answers.

The thing that I test most rigorously when I interview is a candidate's listening skills. I will run him or her through exercises that, if he or she is not paying absolute attention to what's going on, he or she will fail miserably. Success in sales has much more to do with listening than talking.

Developing a Sales Team & Setting Goals

How to Form a Successful Sales Team

To have a successful sales team, it is important to execute a multi-point strategy. Number one, hire "great athletes." Specialists typically are good within their areas of expertise but are limited in their abilities to grow into other areas. Those with good skills across several disciplines (communication, assessment, quantification and problem solving) have the ability to be successful in many areas.

As was note previously, the most important skill area is communications. Many times, when people hear the term "communication skills," they think speaking and writing. While speaking and writing skills are important, the most important communication skill is listening.

The critical skills area is the ability to provide assessment and qualification. Individuals that are able to rapidly assess the opportunities and validate whether they have an option that fits the needs of the customer are typically the most successful sales executives. There is a natural tendency to over estimate the value and probability of closing any opportunity. The representative that is able to avoid time-wasting opportunities by keeping them out of his or her pipeline and focusing on the real opportunities is able to close more business.

The next area is problem solving and quantitative skills. That's usually the area of greatest need in any sales organization. The more complex the product and target market, the more valuable are the skills of problem solving. Being able to identify and qualify options to any situation, the more likely the chance of finding the right option for the opportunity. In most cases, one's ability to quantify those options, either financially or technically, is directly tied to the ability to identify the "right" solution out of many options. We're selling a very capital-intensive solution. Our average sales price can range, depending on a given time, between $200,000 per sale to as high as $4 million. So, you better be able to position something in terms of a return on investment strategy.

The success of the sales leader is dependant upon his or her ability of marrying the right people with the right skills to the correct market and account base. A market and client profile that has a high capital or real estate investment is going to require sales representatives that are comfortable in using spreadsheets as a primary tool in identifying and proposing the best solution for the opportunity. It's matching up the right skill set and people with the needs of the account base.

The role of "rainmaker" is a role that every sales representative strives to obtain. Time, superior skills and right market opportunity are the requirements to become this highest class of sales representative. The ability of any individual to maintain his or her dedication and energy while growing to become the next rainmaker is critical. It's hiring people that have that type of resilience and self-confidence, and the ability to believe, "Yes, I'm new in role, I'm new in territory. The rainmaker has been there for a long time and has a very established account base. If given a similar amount of time, I'm going to do as well or better than what the rainmaker is doing."

When it comes to goals, there are two areas of focus. The first is a strong focus on the company revenue and income objectives. Metrics of "revenue," "net revenue," "net income," "gross/net margin" and "days sales outstanding" are typically the metrics that drive any compensation plan, and then the plan drives the behavior of the sales team.

The second area would be determined based on defined strategic initiatives. There might be a piece of business that, financially, is worth a value of X, but because it hits directly a new area of the market or the weakness of a competitor, the value of that business is actually greater than X.

Creating goals and compensation plans based on these two principles borders on alchemy. The empirical side of the equation notes that a given type of revenue drives a certain level of profit, and that profit will support a commission rate within the cost of sales. The magic is in adjusting goals and compensation to emphasize a strategy that, while might not be as profitable, is in the best interest of the company.

Sales Manager Challenges

The number one challenge for any sales leader is always meeting the company's objectives. It is more effective in the long term to accomplish this goal with a cohesive team that is willing to work together, as opposed to herding a bunch of individualists. A team that's able to work together and leverage each other's strengths is much more effective organization than a collection of individuals who work in isolation.

Every sales manager is going to face the reoccurring challenge of keeping his or her team highly motivated. It is always "the most important month/quarter/year in the history of company ABC." Financial compensation only goes so far for so long. An individual has to feel like he or she is growing and advancing as a professional, as opposed to just getting a bigger and bigger commission check. Maintaining the growth of the individual over a broad range of professional areas describes that basic challenge. He or she has to make his or her number, but the individual has to feel like he or she is growing as an individual to stay strong.

In developing an individual sales representative's career path, the manager is able to access areas that either interest the sales person or complements his or her role. By encouraging him or her to participate and contribute in other areas, the sales representative may become more effective in his or her area of primary responsibility, as well as contributing to other organizations. An example of this strategy is seen when sales works in partnership with product marketing. The sales representative is able to give specific market insight to marketing and, in the process, become more familiar with the strategy, objectives and capabilities of product offerings. By exposing sales to other areas of the company, the sales organization is able to have a positive contribution outside of sales, as well as gaining skills and knowledge that benefit individuals in the sales role.

The "Sales Star"

When sales star wants a promotion to manager, it is very important to review with them that the typical promotion from "sales star" to "sales manager" usually results in a loss of income. Someone who is the number one sales person is often making significantly more than the management layer above them. There is a misconception that advancement to sales management means a significant increase of income.

A sales person has great control over his or her individual contribution and results. When becoming a sales manager, one only has influence over a group of individuals. It's a significant challenge to suddenly realize that you're not managing yourself, but you're managing the activities of many others. What may have worked for you does not necessarily work for them. This loss of control is sometimes a challenge within the role of manager that aggressive and driven personalities are unable to address.

A great example of this was Irvin "Magic" Johnson. Johnson was a great player for the Los Angeles Lakers and was an NBA coach for all of one week. He became so frustrated trying to coach a "new generation" of players and trying to turn them into what he believed defined success in the past. He was not able to force them to change or adapt to their strengths and personalities, and, as a result, he left that role very quickly.

There are many other roles that can be added to a sales person's responsibilities to give him or her fulfillment beyond simply closing and booking business. While generating profitable revenue is a sale person's primary focus, he or she could have a role with marketing as a liaison between the product marketing requirements process and the actual voice of market. Sales people can also contribute as mentors, not only in sales, but in other areas of the company.

Creating a Team

First, hire people who are naturally very competitive and strive for excellence. Those who have competitive sports in their background or some passionate interest have internalized the process of working harder than is generally expected. That determination is critical in the personality of a successful sales person.

Second, hire a diversity of people. A group of people with differing backgrounds and perspectives, when challenged, are able to contribute many differing approaches to attack that challenge.

Then, finally, find people willing to be part of a team and have some understanding and commitment to the goals of the team. Individual event track stars are different from basketball players. The track star is typically most motivated by the unshared glory of his or her achievement. The football player is accustomed to making sacrifices for the good of the team but always striving to win. Team-oriented personality tends to equate to greater long-term success.

Compensation methodology must not inhibit, but rather place emphasis on, reward for accomplishing the team objective. Simply linking a percentage of the individual's bonus or commissions to the performance of the team enables that incentive. If the individual performs at 125 percent of plan, and the team goals are only 80 percent of plan attainment, individuals might be paid on a scale of 110 percent of plan. The inverse would be the individual that performs at 125 percent of plan being a part of a team that performs at 110 percent of plan. In this case, paying the individual and attainment equal 135 percent of plan motivates an individual to act in the best interest of the team, as well as his or her own personal success. The benefit to an organization is the creation of team commitment. Synergies and strengths are sought between members to accomplish goals.

Preventing Sales Burnout

"Burnout" is a broad term. To understand the issue, you have to look at what is "burning" someone out. Is it boredom? Somebody could be 200 percent of plan and bored to death. Is it frustration? ("I don't have the tools I need. I don't have the products I need.") Is it lack of skills? Are salespeople running into the same problem every day? It's really about understanding what's behind the burnout and addressing that, as opposed to a blanket cure for anybody with burnout. Sending somebody on a club trip is not necessarily the way to fix it.

Once the issue is understood, proactive plans can be created to address the needs of the representative. The bored representative might just need a rotation of territory or market focus. The frustrated representative needs the opportunity to not only identify and communicate his or her frustration, but to become a part of addressing the issues causing frustration (put the representative in charge of the project to define marketing collateral requirements). Once these issues are understood, they can be proactively addressed.

Conclusion

Sales is the most rewarding role in any organization. It touches all external and internal audiences and is the driving force behind almost every successful company. Nothing really happens until the sale is made. It is, typically, the most financially rewarding role within organizations. The opportunity to succeed, measured against quantifiable objectives, is an incredible motivation to those driven to success.

As we move to the future and the industry of HSIA for the hospitality industry, the role of sales will continue to evolve. Strategies and products will adapt to the changing requirements of the market. Competitors will continue to make the market more difficult, either through discounting and behavior out of desperation or aggressive threats from dominant telecommunications providers. Regardless of those changes, sales will continue to be the front line of "providing the customers with what they want, when they want it, at a price they are willing to pay."

Michael Z. Jones is a noted contributor to numerous sales and hospitality industry related articles. Under his leadership, the STSN sales organization has enabled STSN to grow at a rate of more than 75 percent annually during the past two years. Deloitte Touche has subsequently recognized STSN as #3 on the list of the Technology Fast 500. His comments on the complexities of channels and strategic sales methodologies have been the topics of many industry articles.

Mr. Jones joined STSN as senior vice president of sales in November 2002. He has served in numerous leadership roles with several high tech industry leaders. Before joining STSN, he was senior vice president of sales and business development for BlueStep, Inc., a provider of Internet-based collaboration technologies. Prior to BlueStep, Mr. Jones was responsible for the corporate-wide Internet strategy and various operational and sales organizations within Iomega Corporation during the company's period of unprecedented growth. Earlier positions include sales management positions with Silicon Graphics and Oracle Corporation.

Mr. Jones received his B.A. from the University of Utah.

Dedication: *To my current and past sales teams.*

Striking the Right Balance in the Wireless Industry

Michael A. Grollman
Chairman & CEO
National Scientific Corporation

Working in Wireless

We are a small, aggressive public company with roots in semiconductor design for wireless technologies. In 2002, we began focusing on integrated embedded solutions for wireless markets, particularly location-based devices using industry standards like Wi-Fi and GPS.

As CEO, I have three primary responsibilities. My number one job is to increase and improve shareholder value over time. Second, I have a responsibility to find and execute against a value proposition to customers. Third, I need to ensure that the value proposition evolves over time, so that I can increase the number of customers we serve and deliver an improved value proposition to shareholders.

The most difficult thing about providing leadership in a wireless company, or any emerging technologies firm for that matter, is working without a lot of market data to go on. We are working, to some extent, with unknowns; these are new technologies and new applications being brought to new markets. Categorizing what the real value proposition is for customers is a work in progress at all times. Getting this wrong is easy and natural. Getting it right is essential for survival.

Value to Our Customers

One value we provide is in the form of alternative solutions for outdoor or indoor location of people and things in hospitals, for example. We take a wireless standard and provide a data transport infrastructure. Many hospitals have already implemented a Wi-Fi infrastructure for the purpose of patient care. We take that same wireless system, in this case, a Wi-Fi 802.11a/g/b/n network, and use it for additional purposes. We can implement an indoor wireless location system of people and things using the same existing wireless network.

We believe that deploying a proprietary-type of solution can result in a 40 to 50 percent cost advantage to a health care organization. This type of solution fits better with long-term IT infrastructure plans, especially for mid- to large-size health care organizations. This technology allows hospitals to reduce costs and improve patient care at once, since they can find the people and assets they need instantly, improving system efficiency.

This technology would also be beneficial in large manufacturing plants, particularly those with a mix of indoor and outdoor tracking. For example, in automobile manufacturing, you have a flow-through supply chain, and you want to be able to establish position indoors and outdoors. If this company already has a Wi-Fi wireless network for data transportation or is thinking of getting one, our Wi-Fi tracking system can be added at no additional infrastructure cost. The company's initial investment dollars in a Wi-Fi system are now stretched because the same network can support an indoor positioning and location system too, thus getting more bang for their infrastructure investment buck. We also have a version of a Wi-Fi tracking device that has embedded GPS technology. A car that is being moved through a manufacturing plant travels from indoor to outdoor space. The vehicle will pick up a GPS signal once it moves outdoors. This combined technology allows for the car to be monitored and located, whether it is indoors or outdoors.

Our biggest challenge is getting customers to adopt our technology early. If we can get them excited about early-stage deployments, we can create momentum that results in growth and increased revenue through continued adoption of the technologies we are developing.

In more mature industries, you usually have substantial data about what customers want and why they want it; that's a much different scenario than trying to create something that doesn't exist from scratch. When you are providing businesses with cutting-edge technologies, you are also providing them with new information. For example, we try to help hospitals assess how a new technology or product can add value to the businesses they are conducting. How does knowing where a piece of hospital equipment is at any given time affect the hospital's bottom line? What's the true return on investment (ROI) for that piece of information? How important is it for a nurse to be able to find an IV pump in thirty seconds, rather than five or ten minutes?

Because you're dealing with a lack of data with new technologies, it's best to put early-stage tools and pilots into customers' hands and collect real-world information. This type of rapid prototyping approach is key when you want to get early data and make good decisions about where research and development should be headed.

For example, in the case of school buses, we tested the first version of our vehicle telematics technology last year. We ran two pilot programs and gathered feedback on what customers liked or didn't like about it. We then put in place a second pilot program that incorporated some of that feedback. Finally, we ran a third pilot program that included changes we made based on information we gathered from the previous two programs, including a new outstanding remote video function that we learned about only by working with real world customers side by side.

Applications of Wireless Technologies

We market our consumer products through organizations such as Home Shopping Network and QVC; everything else we do is B-to-B or B-to-government transactions.

Our Gotcha!(R) child safety product is designed so that consumers can put it to use immediately. In this case, it uses RFID wireless technology to keep parents and children within a certain distance of each other in crowded places, like shopping malls or the park. The safety device consists of two parts, one carried by the parent and one clipped onto the child.

The parent determines the distance the two units can be from one another before the child unit alarms. While the device is not intended to find lost children, it is an effective aide in preventing them from becoming lost. To date, we have been successful in selling the technology across multiple major retail channels, including HSN and QVC, and we have recently expanded our market into Canada.

To further promote a new technology such as this, two things need to occur: first, we need to learn what customers like and don't like about the product and modify it accordingly. Second, we have to determine in which markets the product has strongest appeal. For example, we've learned that the technology's adoption rate by grandparents is much greater than we ever expected. We also discovered that parents of special needs children are very interested in this technology. We need to listen carefully the needs of various markets if we want to see growth for our products.

Challenges

A wireless company needs to strike a balance between what its core technology is and how much it wants to customize a product for a particular customer application. One of the most significant difficulties with early technology is the long sales cycle. You have to demonstrate not only that your solution is technically sound, but that the information it produces will bring a viable return to a company's business. That means you need to convince both the technology and business people within an organization that the product is worthwhile. You have to successfully convey to them that the information they will acquire by using wireless technology merits the effort and expense needed to implement it in a pilot and, eventually, we hope, a production platform.

When dealing with new technology, there is much more of a learning cycle for early customers. For example, if you are going to sell a backhoe to a construction company, that company already has a good idea of what backhoes do. Convincing them to buy your backhoe is more about features and benefits of your brand than about the need for the machine itself.

From our perspective, we would try to sell a construction company embedded wireless tracking, so that it knows where its backhoes are at any given time and whether or not people are stealing them from the construction site. They may not have thought about this issue before, so we have to convince them that your wireless technology is sound and that the new information offers them a strong value proposition. In other words, they will want to see a good return of investment in a reasonable period of time. With new wireless products, you have to invest more energy and resources into the sales cycle.

Finding Growth Areas and New Customers

We are looking towards advancing this technology—especially in the bus and truck arena—into more powerful computing engines that are mobile. We want to leverage industry standards, both on the communications side, as well as the operating system side, such as Linux and .Net, in order to create highly scalable, very powerful and cost effective computers that can be carried by transportation devices, like buses and trucks.

Locations-based technology is still at a very nascent stage; as a result, looking at existing markets in existing customer-adoption rates is an unreliable predictor of where the markets are going to evolve. We try to provide a variety of different early-stage solutions for customers to try in prototype. We then focus our research and development efforts where we find the greatest customer interest to be.

The Technology Development Process

When you're producing wireless technology, the two most important resources are the technical talent and the tools, such as interface of hardware, software and embedded technologies. It's critical that you establish goals and guidelines for the development process; timelines can get away from you, especially when you're dealing with hardware and software problems. You need goals that will drive the team to produce results within a specific timeframe.

Vehicle Telematics

We have a vehicle telematics-type application, particularly targeted at school buses. This technology tracks children getting on and off school buses using GPS technology. We also have technologies that facilitate the relaying of that information back to servers, so that schools can keep accurate records on where their students are. We complement this with advanced video technology that helps schools know what is happening at any given time on their buses.

There are three reasons why schools would have an interest in knowing who is riding on the school buses and where they get on and off. First, it's important to know where students are. If students don't get off the bus at the right stop, a school would be able to tell parents, with some degree of certainty, where their child *did* get off.

There is also more of a hard-dollar business reason for being able to maintain accurate records on who is using a school transportation system from the point of view of federal reimbursement and other types of programs that help schools financially. From that perspective, it's important for schools to be able to produce good information on how their transportation systems are used.

Finally, protecting children from bullying by others, and keeping a good evidentiary record when it does occur, helps to keep children safe when they ride the bus. A special bonus of our Travedo technology system here is its ability to send each parent an SMS message on his or her cell phone, letting the parent know exactly when his or her child has arrived either safely at school or safely at the home bus stop.

Vehicle telematics technology is also beneficial in the general transportation sector, particularly for companies that operate fleets of trucks and trailers. These businesses have an interest in collecting information regarding where a truck is and where it has been. This technology can also be used to measure tire pressure, the speed of the truck and the driver's hours to make sure that they are in compliance with federal law. Companies are able to report accurately to the government that the drivers are doing what they are supposed to be doing.

Wi-Fi Tracking

A major issue in health care space is cost containment and being able to deliver high-quality health care without continuing to see significant annual increases in the cost of delivering services. To keep costs down, large hospitals and campus-based health care delivery organizations are looking more and more to improve asset utilization.

Today, many hospitals are purchasing very expensive equipment in large quantities to make sure that it is always available to them. If hospitals can take a particular piece of equipment and locate it more quickly for maintenance and care-delivery purposes, then they improve their asset utilization. The overall result is greater efficiency in delivering high-quality care. The goal of our tracking solution for Wi-Fi in a health care environment is to enable a facility to find equipment in a hurry and in real time.

Benefits and Drawbacks of Partnering

There is a great deal of complexity in building end-to-end wireless solutions. In order to make your way through that maze, you need a diverse group of core competencies. In a smaller company especially, that spectrum of core competencies is very expensive to hold in-house at all times.

By partnering with other companies, you can skip over some areas that are not your specialty. We gain some of these same benefits by cooperating fully with the Linux Open Source community. But the downside of partnering is a loss of control over the overall quality and delivery of a solution. If your partner doesn't get something done on time, the overall solution could be at risk. Partnering is useful for enabling the product development side to focus on just that—development—but it creates a risk in terms of overall delivery if you don't choose your partners carefully.

Characteristics of an Effective Team

When putting together an effective team within your company, it's important to look for people with complementary skills and attitudes. Because we focus on the embedded wireless space technologies, we look for engineers and software developers with skills in those areas. It's helpful if they have some insight into how radios work and how hardware and software come together in embedded space.

In terms of sales and marketing, it's important to have people on board with a track record of working with a particular type of customer and that can bring those established relationships with them. That relationship-building process is one of the most time-consuming aspects of the sales cycle, especially in large infrastructure sales. But it is also important when working with new-customer markets to have sales people that can build new relationships and listen to customer feedback. The feedback they provide can help the research and development department effectively improve the product over time.

At the same time, you don't want to get caught in the trap of constantly selling tomorrow's products. Finding sales people that can strike that balance is always a challenge. You want to look for people that are comfortable with a dynamic that involves dealing with customers that want one thing today and something else tomorrow.

Setting Goals

The goals for the company team are the same as the overall goals for the company: get product into the hands of customers who will help us push it through the optimization and development process. Your goals should be organized around acquisition of new customers, new pilots and the achievement of different development milestones, from early prototyping until late prototyping. But early pilots do not feed cash flow, as a rule. The solution must evolve into something customers will demand and pay a fair price for in the open market.

Another goal is to produce specific technology results from different states of prototyping and early product release. You want to be able to show improvements in the products as they get more and more mature.

On the technology side, having a fairly disciplined testing regimen is important. In addition, having good product specifications—both at a functional level and at the level of internal specification detail—is useful for keeping things on track.

The sales cycle is an art more than a science, but you can certainly measure things, like the number of leads you are working on and the number of pilots you have operating, at any given point in time. The final goal is to generate revenue and profits as a result of that activity.

Staying Connected, Keeping Current

It's important to review trade periodicals and to be engaged with the overall industry network through tradeshows and seminars. These venues offer an exchange of information in both direct and indirect ways. I think spending time with customers and developers is also a good way to stay in touch with the latest news and techniques.

For tracking the electronics industry in general, good tools include *Embedded Systems Journal*, *Wireless News*, *Wireless Developer*, and trade shows and scientific sessions. Events I enjoy include CITA, on the technology side, and ION meetings for the wireless location science information. Some of the large consumer electronics shows are very helpful and interesting as well, such as CES. It's also a good idea to consult with business and technical advisory people from the educational, scientific and business communities. They can help you set direction and strategy with better perspective.

As a wireless company, one of the biggest challenges you face is attracting sufficient capital to develop products quickly enough, so that you can build revenue momentum. There is always a balance between getting things out quickly, building the revenue and attracting capital to help build the next generation of innovative and salable products. The effective combination of all three into a virtuous circle of these things will keep your company on the cutting edge of the wireless industry, which, at times, seems almost to be changing day to day.

Michael A. Grollman is the chairman and chief executive officer of National Scientific Corporation, a publicly-traded technology firm focused on wireless location-sensing products and semiconductor IP. Prior to joining NSC in September 2000, Mr. Grollman served as regional service director of MicroAge, Inc., a company that provides customer-configured technology solutions to businesses. He served as general manager, executive vice president and chief technology officer for Advanced Information Systems from 1987 to 1998.

Mr. Grollman received his Bachelor of Science degree in chemistry from the State University of New York. He received his M.B.A. from Arizona State University and is currently working on a Ph.D. in business and applied computer science from Northcentral University.

Developing Wi-Fi

Todd Myers
CEO
Airpath Wireless, Inc.

Wi-Fi Ubiquity

Our software technologies make public wireless Internet access (Wi-Fi hotspots) easy for an end-user to use and profitable for service providers that own hotspot networks. Airpath's customers are hotspot service providers. These providers design, build and maintain their hotspot networks, antennas and other associated equipment within a location, such as a hotel, airport or convention facility. Once a location for Wi-Fi access has been chosen and contracts with a service provider, it connects the deployed network to our hosted software platforms through the Internet using its choice of equipment (a hotspot gateway). Once the gateway is configured with our systems through an easy-to-use Web interface, the provider uses our software to manage the branding, billing and roaming elements for the hotspot(s).

When service providers utilize our applications, they also become members of the Airpath Provider Alliance. The best way to describe our alliance network is to compare it to the ATM banking networks, where the bank is comparable to a service provider and the Airpath Provider Alliance is the intermediary network, like Cirrus or Plus. While you travel outside of your home banking location, your ATM card can be used in most other global ATMs because Cirrus and Plus link the networks together. They act as a central brand and an interconnect point that transmits the ATM card information to your local bank, which allows you to draw cash. In a similar vein, Airpath manages the information flow between Wi-Fi hotspot providers by handling the clearing transactions between the owners of the hotspot and the service provider that end-users choose for their Wi-Fi account. The Airpath Provider Alliance network allows the end-user to use his or her account information at any affiliated hotspot globally. Airpath's software also handles all of the settlement services behind the scenes and represents the networks to larger carriers.

The Players

In the wireless LAN industry, the people and entities that are involved are service providers, venues, end-users and companies, like ours, that operate behind the scenes. The people who install and operate a wireless network are the service providers. Service providers generally install the equipment, own the infrastructure and manage the end-users. We offer the service provider a set of hosted software applications that help it operate its business without heavy investment in back-end infrastructure.

Venues are the locations where hotspots are installed for public access use. For example, you may have stayed at a "Wi-Fi-enabled" hotel. Service providers generally negotiate revenue-sharing contracts with venues and manage the hotspot for the property. In addition to individual venues, many cities are becoming Wi-Fi enabled through federal funding dollars to support economic development or rural broadband initiatives (like Nantucket).

Since the Wi-Fi industry is changing rapidly, we continuously update our software applications and provide the latest tools to service providers based on industry trends and end-user demand, such as new voice-over IP and content over broadband services.

A Fragmented Industry

From the end user perspective, the industry is fragmented in that many locations are not Wi-Fi ready, the login process is cumbersome,] and prices vary from free to up to $20 per day. If you have wireless access at your office, wouldn't it be nice to use your network username and password as you traveled for business in the airport or hotel? Wouldn't it also be nice to know that you wouldn't have to pay additional roaming fees or setup three separate accounts as you traveled? This is an example of the current fragmentation in the marketplace that Airpath is addressing.

Due to the fragmentation, ad-hoc users are the most prevalent in today's public Wi-Fi hotspots. Ad-hoc users choose to utilize Wi-Fi services at a property but only want to pay for services on an hour-by-hour or day-by-day basis. These ad-hoc users are, generally, not willing to commit to an unlimited subscription for Wi-Fi services because there aren't enough locations to use the service to justify a monthly recurring fee. Many venues have installed Wi-Fi networks that address the short-term ad-hoc user, but they haven't planned for the inevitable mass adoption of Wi-Fi, which creates additional market fragmentation.

Capitalizing on the Problems

Airpath makes money by forecasting and analyzing where the problems in the industry are and creating tools and services that answer the demand. We've created tools that help service providers manage the ad-hoc users for the short-term and have tools available for them for handling more complex billing and promotional services in the future. For example, a service provider uses our application to help it centrally manage a hotspot network in twelve hotels. We allow the service provider to generate coupon numbers, so a front-desk can issue them to guests that are checking into a hotel. If the guest doesn't have a coupon number, we allow a user to enter his or her credit card in to access the location. In addition, if an end-user visits the hotel and already has a Wi-Fi account through an affiliated service provider, we handle the roaming and settlement fees.

Since the Wi-Fi hotspot industry is fairly new, there wasn't any software that focused on the current and future needs of the service providers. We created and host the software tools to help them capitalize on the business. By "hosting" the software, we operate as a service bureau, which saves our customers the intense capital required to the back-office elements of a hotspot.

The Role of the CEO

As the CEO and president, I have the task of guiding the company in the direction that, through strategic planning, increases value to the shareholders. The strategic issues usually involve watching industry trends, analyzing customer suggestions and just simply forward thinking by putting myself in the "customer's shoes." In addition, I also talk to analysts and reporters to find out what they think tomorrow will bring and to share our vision. Of course, working with the management team is extremely important as well. By having proactive dialogues, sharing and determining our visions and agreeing on a budget to help us achieve our objectives, we can allocate the resources needed to execute our plans.

Another role is to evaluate companies that may be complimentary to our core business objectives and determine if there may be an acquisition candidate. I look for companies that could enhance our services and our customer-base. I also look for those that have the ability to increase the overall value of the company and make recommendations to the board based on corporate and investment objectives. We're currently looking at potential opportunities that will expand our global presence.

One of the biggest difficulties I face is keeping up with the pace of the industry and making sure that my team is working as fast. I've been involved as an executive in the technology industry for the past fifteen years, so I'm used to working, as I say, "in dog-years."

Financial Impact

I spend a considerable amount of my time on finances. I suggest to my management team areas in which to budget their departments' costs and revenues. I suggest ways to increase margins, and I make pricing and service offering recommendations that always keeps us ahead of the competition. A key element to our financial success has been the use of automation to operate repetitive parts of the business, such as marketing and accounting, without losing the ultra-important human element.

Executive Relationships

I work closely with other leaders in our industry to help guide standards and to share some of the trends. I also keep in touch with various financial organizations, and I'm in constant contact with strategic partners and customers so I understand their needs. Their input is invaluable when creating and measuring the overall success of our objectives.

Employee Qualities

My management team is tasked with hiring and coordinating the efforts of their respective departments, so everyone is meeting the overall company objectives. My VPs were hired based on several factors:

- Executive experience: Can this person build and manage a team that will perform the execution of the strategy?

- Industry expertise: Does this person know the industry, the players in the industry, and will they help the credibility of the company?
- Personality: Will this person be dynamic and strengthen the overall atmosphere, so everyone in the company feels like they have a voice in the direction? We look for people that have a "roll-up the sleeves" mentality and people that know how to put the customer and the revenue objectives first.

Situations

There are many situations where a CEO must carefully consider the choices he or she makes when leading the company in terms of how to keep the company moving forward.

Increasing Revenue by 25 Percent Over the Next Year

I would start by identifying if the market can support 25 percent revenue growth. If it can, I would engage the team to brainstorm on ways to capture the market, such as: What types of people do these prospects do business with? Can we build relationships with companies that have already built a relationship with our prospect? If the market couldn't support it, I would engage the team to help identify complimentary markets to help us create a plan to continually build the business. Our customer-base is usually the best source to find new markets. Spending thirty minutes every quarter on the phone with your top customers goes a long way!

Losing a Key Employee

First of all, proactively, I make sure I know (in general) how to take on every role should I need to fill the position while we're seeking a replacement. For example, a principal in a high school should, generally, knows how to teach a class if a teacher is out. I try to be ready for the same thing. I also proactively maintain a set of resumes and have positions documented as much as possible.

Our dream is to continue to lead our market, increase profits and ultimately execute on an exit strategy that is profitable for the investors and employees. I keep my edge by being able to think ahead of the curve and more importantly, listening closely to our partners and customers.

Reading Advice for New Employees

I recommend many on-line industry resources, such as *802.11 Planet.com* and *The 802.11 Report.* These on-line resources are critical to our success because the news is up to the second. These and others supply valuable insight on industry trends, and it allows us to analyze the competitive landscape.

I also recommend that employees read *Why Good Companies Go Bad.* It is a great book because it uses a common-sense approach to create a better workplace for themselves through team-building.

Best Piece of Advice

I tell others because I have been told the following: Have a plan and a vision and a way to pay for them. I also tell people to make sure there is a real marketplace; there must be people willing to buy your product or service.

In addition, I have three golden rules. The first is to listen to your customers. Customers are your asset and they can make or break you if you listen to what they have to say. Next, use common sense. If you wouldn't buy or use something you're selling, why should your customer? And the third golden rule is, of course, "Do Unto Others, As You Would Have Them Do Unto You." This last rule helps to build trusted relationships. Without trust in the customer relationship, you can't make a sale.

Todd Myers founded Airpath Wireless Inc. in 2001 and is the company's chief executive officer. Mr. Myers has a proven track record of creating and managing successful companies. Before founding Airpath, Mr. Myers served as the president and CEO of WholesaleISP, a leading wholesale enabler to ISPs. The company focused on creating Web-based productivity applications and services that allowed ISPs to reduce overhead costs and increase their value proposition. WholesaleISP was acquired in August of 2000.

In 1995, Mr. Myers founded GlassCity Internet and served as president and CEO. GlassCity Internet was one of Ohio's largest Internet Service Providers, the only one with a large-scale deployed wireless broadband network. GlassCity Internet was acquired in 1999 by the largest publicly-traded regional ISP in the Midwest.

Mr. Myers' entrepreneurial experience grows out of his role as co-founder and vice president of Northwest Ohio's largest systems integration company, which installed and maintained computers and networks for the area's leading businesses.

Mr. Myers holds numerous educational certifications and has been recognized and quoted by the media as an expert in the IT, Internet, and Wi-Fi fields. While attending the DeVry Institute of Technology in Los Angeles, Mr. Myers specialized in telecommunications management.

Successfully Riding the Technology Wave

Ken Cranston
President & CEO
Terion

About Terion

Our company, Terion, utilizes GPS (Global Positioning System) and digital cellular technology to locate, monitor, and communicate with an asset, such as a trailer, construction vehicle, tanker or a container. We offer our customers the ability to better utilize their equipment because our device enables them to know where their equipment is at all times. Customers can then become more efficient in how they use that asset. For example, the typical trucking company has three to four trailers for every tractor in its fleet. That translates to 75 percent of their assets not being utilized at any given time, a significant inefficient use of working capital. The reason for this inefficiency is simple; the average trucking company has trouble locating and, therefore, utilizing their trailers that all look virtually the same and are dispersed all over the country.

Primary Clients

Our products target the transportation group, specifically trucking companies, by establishing a critical point of communication with the trailer. Our device provides business-critical information, including location, speed and status information, such as whether or not the trailer is full or empty and whether or not the doors have been opened or closed. We collect the data and transmit it from the trailer back to a central location. The trucking company can then use that data to make critical business decisions such as the following:

- Sending a driver to this specific location to pick up an empty trailer;
- Booking a load for a customer that has just loaded a trailer and sending a driver to pick it up;
- Moving fifteen trailers from a location not utilizing them to a location that needs more trailers;
- Charging a shipper customer for keeping a trailer longer than was contractually stipulated (called detention charges).

The customer of the trucking company, the shipper, also benefits from our product. Shippers can better manage their dock operations and, ultimately,

Successfully Riding the Technology Wave

the flow of inventory with our technology. They also benefit from improved cargo security. Trailers are, at times, stolen while in-transit, with over a million dollars in cargo on board. The ability to track the trailer and catch the thief in the act is very appealing to the shipper, as well as the trucking company.

The government is also interested in this technology from a homeland security standpoint. Homeland security officials have stated that the next potential terrorist attack could be a trailer loaded with explosives parked near the terrorist target. The ability to monitor such hazardous cargo or restrict its movement can be a significant security advantage. Our technology provides the shipper and/or the trucking company the ability to "lock down" high-value or hazardous freight. If a trailer that has been locked down is moved, the door opened or tampered with, we can proactively send an alarm notification to the security groups e-mail account, pager and mobile phone to allow for immediate action within minutes of the tampering.

Expansion Targets

We have identified three areas where Terion delivers value to our customers. The first two areas we deliver to our customers today. First, we provide tracking capabilities to improve the efficiency in managing mobile assets (basic tracking). Second, we provide for the security of the mobile asset and it's cargo through geo-fencing and advanced sensor capabilities (door sensors, cargo sensors, tractor ID sensors).

The third area of value we are currently developing will leverage the advancement of RFID (radio frequency identification) technologies currently being piloted, which will allow our devices to provide in transit visibility to inventory. This translates to real-time inventory management. We believe that, in the next twelve to twenty-four months, RFID technology will be mature enough to integrate with our product, making the trailer a virtual "moving warehouse." RFID is a technology that is being driven by the Department of Defense, as well as large retailers, such as Wal-Mart. It is believed that the successful development and adoption of RFID technology will eventually replace current UPC codes on all items with RFID tags.

What we envision in the future is that our devices read all pallets/items loaded onto a trailer. As the vehicle is being loaded and/or en-route to its destination, we will transmit information about the contents to the shipper/receiver as necessary. Inventory could then be monitored real-time in-transit and re-directed en route to wherever it is currently needed. For example, if a hot item flying off the shelves at a particular store or town becomes sold out, a retailer could re-direct inventory currently in-transit. Dynamic inventory management maximizes sales revenue, reduces inventory shortages, enhances customer satisfaction and, ultimately, reduces the working capital needs of the shipper.

Growth Areas

As a small start-up company, we focused on creating a market-leading product for the transportation sector. In 2004, we achieved this objective. We currently hold 80 to 85 percent of the market share, with over 84,000 devices currently installed today in a market with more than 4 million trailers. We plan to maintain this advantage through our focus on continuous product and software function ability enhancements, all performed over-the-air without disruption to the customer. As trucking companies/shippers continue to adopt this technology, we are well positioned to maintain our leadership position and add several hundred thousand trailers to our base.

We are also looking at alternative vertical markets that would benefit from our ability to track, monitor and communicate with remote assets. Examples include construction assets, refrigerated trailers that haul our food supply, flatbed trailers and others being discussed. We are also looking at the service supply chain, including utilities, such as the phone company and other local service vehicles that can be managed more efficiently. We will continue evaluating these and other vertical markets and geographies as we further refine and deliver on our mission to help customers drive inefficiencies out of their businesses.

Identifying New Products/Enhancements

We have formalized the process of gathering customer feedback. We regularly solicit customer input to determine product development priorities. Our product development group then prioritizes engineering efforts based on delivering the advancements that provide the most value to our current and targeted customers. Our product has evolved significantly over the years and meets the needs of our target customer better than any competitive offering because of this approach. The net result of this effort is a "best-in-class" product offering and a corresponding increase in our revenue stream, as we charge for new products, capabilities and features.

An example of the benefit of this product development approach involves the development of our patented Cargo Sensor. A few years ago, one of our major customers tasked us with developing a sensor that could accurately determine whether its trailer was loaded or unloaded. This would allow the customer to not only know the location of its trailer, but whether it was empty and available for another load or loaded and ready to book and begin delivering revenue generating miles.

We needed a device that would detect a load anywhere within the fifty-three foot span of the trailer. We found that a single sensor wasn't adequate in capturing the full view of the trailer. We developed an ultrasonic sensor cluster that consists of a short-range sensor for the first ten feet of the trailer, a long-range sensor that looks at the last forty-three feet of the trailer and a proximity sensor that senses freight in the front nose of the trailer. Our engineering group also developed a proprietary algorithm that accurately measures freight activity in the various climates that a trailer and freight is exposed to.

As of today, we are the only company that offers a cargo sensor that works. In fact, every major competitor has contacted Terion to license our Cargo Sensor. We listen and then politely decline.

Going Vertical

We also leverage our customers' knowledge bases as we evaluate expansion into other vertical markets. For example, we have installed our product on roughly 20,000 trailers for one customer that also has an inter-model container division. The customer began evaluating the feasibility of tracking its inter-model containers and solicited our assistance. Several unique issues needed to be addressed before a tracking product for containers could be deployed. We worked closely with the customer to develop a solution that addressed the issues and piloted our prototype solution for a six-month period. The end result was a product that not only met the customer's needs, but also could be marketed to other inter-model container companies. Because of our close relationship with our customers, we see opportunities such as this very frequently.

Educating the Customer

The market that we serve is still in the early stages of adoption. Educating the prospects in this market on the benefits and payback of our technology is challenging at times. Our job is to not only present the specific benefits of our product, but also illustrate the return on investment achieved by deploying this technology. If we can prove to the C-level executives that our product is not an expense, but instead a method to increase efficiency, reduce operating costs, increase revenues and, thereby, generate positive returns, we've made a sale.

The Role of the CEO

As the President and CEO of Terion, Inc., I have a hand in all aspects of the business. We are a young company with forty employees, which requires all of us to wear several hats. I focus primarily on our marketing and sales activities. I assist our sales team on sales calls with our largest prospects and, typically, lead the presentation to these clients. As one would expect, I am also part of the team that goes out and talks to investors about future possibilities for the company, as we are always looking at merger/acquisition type opportunities.

From a financial standpoint, my daily focus is on enhancing the value of our company. We are primarily a venture capital-backed company with a clear goal to create value for our stakeholders. The way we do that is by finding and signing new clients, perfecting our technology and offering new enhancements, so our existing customers and new customers can implement more efficient ways to do business that they never could in the past.

The Players

When we work with a client, we are normally dealing with C-level executives. Typically, we meet with the vice president of operations, the CFO, as well as the president and CEO, because adopting and implementing this efficiency tool is normally considered a large capital expenditure. It can require a capital outlay of anywhere from $100,000 to millions of dollars for the hardware and a monthly recurring charge for the wireless service to deliver the data for decision-making. We typically sign contracts for three to five years, evidencing the commitment that these customers are making to us and vice versa.

The VP of operations is typically looking for ways to become more efficient in his or her operations. We bring in a team to demonstrate our software application, its functionality and how it can help drive inefficiencies out of his or her business. We actually show the VP how the software works in his or her business environment and how it will directly benefit the business. Once the individual or team is sold on the fact that things could be done a little differently and more efficiently, he or she will then involve the CFO and CEO, because they are, typically, going to make the financial decision.

The CFO is someone we work with to develop the return on investment with his or her own assumption set. Once the CFO understands that our product will return his or her capital investment in a twelve to eighteen-month time frame, he or she is typically interested in incorporating the tool into his or her system and daily operations. The president is, then, someone we meet with to convince that we are a viable and stable company that is going to be around and supporting the company in the future. With our leadership team experience and expertise, as well as the excitement and commitment we exude, we are able to overcome any initial concerns that the president may have.

Qualities of an Employee

For an employee to be a valuable asset to us and enjoy working at Terion, he or she must be a bit of a risk taker and be entrepreneurial in spirit. We make it clear to our employees that each and every one of them is critical to our success, and we, therefore, make them owners in the company. Every employee is awarded stock options. It is widely accepted and understood that, at any given time, they may feel compelled by their own drive for success to work a twenty-hour day or a seven-day week in order to get a project done.

Constant communication with the team is important. For one thing, everyone must understand the company vision and goals in order for Terion to be successful. Our vision is to be the leading wireless asset management and technology company, providing wireless location and information solutions that help our customers drive inefficiencies out of their businesses. It is important that everyone "buys-in" to this vision. The combination of understanding and commitment to the company vision and goals is critical to our long-term success.

Goal Setting

We establish extremely lofty goals as a young technology company. We also attempt to set as many quantitative goals as possible. This allows us to readily measure results. For example, everyone in the company knows how many tracking devices we are going to sell for the month or even the year. We also celebrate our achievements together.

Biggest Challenge

Our biggest challenge is maintaining a focus on the few critical goals with the greatest impact; that is, ensuring that our forty employees pursue the tasks that have the most positive impact to our customers and on the value of the business on a daily basis. There is no shortage of great new product enhancement ideas we could develop or large new market verticals that would benefit from our core technology. Becoming distracted on non-critical tasks would lead to poor execution in a small company such as ours.

Prioritization and communication of those priorities is mission-critical for Terion. As I stated previously, regular active communication is the best way to ensure that we are all focused on the same few critical goals. Each department gets together on a weekly basis to review project status and priorities. An all-hands company meeting is held each month to ensure that each department understands the company priorities and how they relate to each department and, ultimately, each individual.

Keeping Your Edge

A significant part of my role in the company is to maintain an external focus on the events and developments outside of the company that may affect Terion. The transportation industry is, typically, a sector that is affected first as the economy declines but is also the first to recover as the economy improves. Keeping track of the leading economic indicators is critical to understanding the relative health of our target customer. Fortunately, the economy is currently strong, and our transportation customers are enjoying very healthy demand for freight shipments. Evaluation and subsequent investment in Terion technology is more likely in good economic times.

I also monitor the issues and government actions related to terrorism and homeland security. Terion's technology helps ensure cargo security today and, I believe, will play a significant role in homeland security initiatives in the future, as the U.S. takes action to secure its supply chain.

The Future of the Wireless Industry

I firmly believe that the next wireless growth segment will involve the combination of GPS location capabilities and a wireless communication device. E-911 initiatives have been delayed for various reasons. The delay notwithstanding, every cell phone will be GPS-enabled in the future. Companies that provide applications developed around wireless GPS tracking, like Terion, will see significant market adoption, as technology advances create increased functionality in smaller form factors at less cost. Ultimately, all remote assets, like cars, trailers, trucks and construction vehicles, will all have GPS tracking devices. The day will come when our parents, children, and even our pets will all be capable of being tracked wirelessly.

Best Piece of Advice

The key to being successful is to communicate effectively and to be consistent and persistent. I think that part of what we have learned at Terion is that it has taken four years for an idea to really come to a point where it is starting to take off. Along the way, there were many opportunities to give up, but, I think if you have a technology, a dream and a vision, you need to be consistent with it and communicate it effectively. Ultimately, you will be successful.

Ken Cranston, president and chief executive officer, joined Terion in 1999, prior to product launch, and brings over eighteen years business experience to the organization. His negotiating abilities have led to strategic alliances with Verizon, J.B. Hunt, XTRA Lease and QUALCOMM. Mr. Cranston has worked with numerous high profile investors to fund the organization. He has been commended throughout his career for motivational abilities, positive attitude and his enthusiasm.

Mr. Cranston started his career at NBC in New York as a business analyst and moved on to various roles at Western Union. After seven successful years at Western Union, he moved on to Telespectrum Worldwide, Inc. as senior vice president of sales and marketing.

Mr. Cranston is a husband, the proud father of four boys, and enjoys an active family life. He received his Bachelor of Arts degree in Economics from Iona College.

Managing a Wireless Network

Greg Murphy
COO & Founder
AirWave Wireless

Landscape of the Wireless Industry

We can divide the wireless industry into six categories. The first category is the manufacturers of wireless enabled devices targeting end users, such as mobile phones. The second category is the infrastructure hardware vendors, such as Cisco or some of the wireless LAN startups that provide the hardware that deliver data to end user devices. The third category can be described as intrusion detectors that ensure the data transmitted between wireless devices is encrypted and secure. This includes authentication and access control. In this same category are the tools to determine when networks are under attack by detecting any unauthorized users accessing the network.

The fourth category is one that we fall in, network management. Once you've got that wireless infrastructure in place with thousands of wireless devices, you are faced with the enormous challenge of managing, monitoring and ensuring that the performance of the network is adequate. The IT organization has the ability to control the network and implement policies, as well as reconfigure the network to maintain optimal performance.

The fifth category is end user device management. There is enormous difficulty with configuring all types of wireless devices to connect to wireless networks. These devices need to be configured properly to connect effectively. This is a growing category, allowing companies to implement policies for all users on the network. In this same category, we also see specialized software for roaming. The last category encompasses wireless service providers, which can range from managed service providers that operate and maintain wireless networks to traditional ISPs building hot spots, connecting to networks in cafes, to the largest wireless companies serving the enterprise space, such as T-Mobile, Sprint and so on.

The Search for the Holy Grail

In wireless technology, the Holy Grail is the convergence of voice and data networks. We are looking at enormous possibilities when you can deliver data to phones and use your WLAN technologies to deliver low cost, affordable mobile voice. The challenge is to ensure that the systems are in place to manage and control those networks. Look back to the early days of cellular phones. Think about the systems in the late 1980s, when the quality was abysmal. To achieve ubiquity with wireless voice, wireless networks have to deliver the same quality users came to expect on traditional voice networks.

Determining Growth Areas

The way we determine where growth areas will be is by talking to the people who are responsible for maintaining and installing these wireless networks. We examine the problems they are experiencing. Network management is a huge issue for network administrators, and we talk to an array of these administrators, some of whom are experienced in managing Ethernet networks and are now in charge of wireless networks. This involves radio frequency networks that they've never managed before. We talk to these network administrators about the problems associated with their wireless networks, trying to solve those problems. We can draw on the analogy of the Ma Bells in the 1950s and putting them in charge of AT&T Wireless, with RF interference issues. It's a whole different world with a new set of needs. The way you really understand the issues is by talking to the folks that are responsible for those networks. They can identify where the problems are.

Problems and Misconceptions

The biggest problem the industry has, really, relates to security and manageability. One of the biggest misconceptions in the industry is that they are two separate problems, when they are two sides of the same coin. One relates to protecting your data, and the other relates to configuring and controlling the network infrastructure itself. The network cannot be secure if you don't have the ability to manage it. In your home, you can put in the best burglar alarm system, but, if you don't have a system in place to lock everything, that alarm system won't do you a lot of good. The security needs to be taken care of, while managing and enforcing the policies uniformly are just as important and can be tremendously difficult. Thousands of potential intrusions are possible on a wireless network. Managing wireless networks is a lot more complicated than managing a wired network that contains a defined number of points through which people can access. On a wireless network, there are an infinite number of places where intruders can access your network.

Biggest Frustrations

One of the biggest frustrations is found in one of the areas that also holds the most excitement, dealing with new technologies. With new technologies often comes the difficult job of educating the market as to potential problems. This includes folks like industry analysts and the press. The biggest challenge is having them understand new technology and the ways in which it will affect the industry. The other side of operating in a small company environment means you have to continuously be out there, convincing people that your company is viable, that it will be around in one or two or three years. One of the unfortunate legacies of 1999 and the Internet bubble is that many customers ended up buying products that disappeared. Once customers have been burned, they are reluctant to buy from a small company. The only way you overcome that is by building better products than your larger counterparts.

Job Responsibilities

As the COO and founder of AirWave Wireless, one of my primary goals is to build products that solve real problems. I want to make it easy for users to take advantage of that product, and everything else flows from that. To make the company increasingly profitable, we need to have products that meet the needs of customers and that are easy for them to use. I start with the customers and build products that meet their needs.

Another component of my job is taking a strategic look at the industry and listening to how people want to use wireless technology in the future. We then translate customers' needs into specific products. To anticipate the types of problems they will encounter, we listen to users' immediate concerns and make sure we understand where they are heading over the next period of years.

I also have to ensure that we focus on quality. We conduct extensive reviews of the products we are developing to ensure they have been thoroughly tested. We are not asking customers to experiment on our behalf. This is critical in the enterprise market. We also are building the right relationships and partnerships, which are particularly critical in the management space. We need to ensure that multiple systems can communicate and interoperate with one another. The focus is not just on our products, but also on putting them in place, and that means interoperability.

Daily Contacts

I work most closely with our chief executive officer, as well as with our VP of sales and marketing. I work with the marketing organization and our teams in product development and the finance group, making sure we are performing well as a company. Obviously, I spend as much time as I can with customers, partners, and distributors. One of the things I want to emphasize is that our company is not far removed from direct contact with customers. That is one of my favorite things about a startup company. There are few layers of management between us and the customer; that makes us nimble and responsive to customer needs.

Job Skills

The skills that have served me best in this dynamic industry are constant innovation and maintaining a realistic view of an industry that shifts from day to day. We operate in an unforgiving industry that demands performance. When a customer puts the management of its wireless network in your hands, there is no option but to deliver the best product in the industry. Doing that takes an enormous amount of planning and constant innovation to add features that will resolve current and future issues as your customer's wireless network grows.

Skills for a Prospective Employee

We are mostly looking for people who have a combination of intelligence and flexibility. The ability to adapt is critical in a small company environment, where people often wear a lot of different hats. We look for a great attitude and a great customer focus. Employees must enjoy working with customers.

Making Money

Our company makes money by licensing software to end users, working with distributors and system integrators. A lot of partners are selling to end user customers. We also make money by upgrading our product and continuously adding innovative new features. As our customer networks grow, their needs become greater and greater.

The other side of making money is controlling our expenses. Our two major areas of expense are research and development. We build the product and then market and sell it.

Setting and Executing Goals

At the top level, we focus on what we are setting out to accomplish with the business. We have innovative products and are targeting specific revenue. We set goals for our engineering product team. We have to figure out how to sell those products, and that creates a set of goals for the sales team. We work collaboratively as a management team, where we set short-term goals on how to move forward in the next quarter, and then establish goals for the long term.

In general, we try to always figure out where we want to drive the organization, using quantifiable metrics that include the number of customers we want to have, the resellers and partners we want to have and what the average product price should be. It's a simple matter of translating the goals and making each executive and manager responsible for figuring out how he or she will achieve those goals. We hire good people, tell them what the company needs to accomplish and give them the freedom to figure out how they are going to achieve those goals. One thing we try to avoid is setting too many different goals. We see other organizations that drive themselves crazy trying to execute too many goals simultaneously. It is more effective to set three or four top goals and quantify them. Setting a list of twenty-five strategic objectives leaves everyone confused.

The Bottom Line

One facet of my job that directly contributes to the company's bottom line is my active participation in all of our product development processes. Having products on the market drives increased revenue to the company. We believe in the value we provide with product innovation. There is an initial investment in the technology, in the form of the research and development budget. Once we build the product, we determine how to get it out there, via partners, in order to reduce our distribution costs on a day-to-day basis. We have to continue to work on pricing. Simply put, revenue equals price times quantity. If the pricing is right and the distribution strategy is in place, we can deliver our product and meet our goals.

Effective product development involves the entire company. In a small organization, everyone has a really high level of responsibility. Everyone in the organization, from engineers to support salesmen, they can all directly see how they are affecting the company as a whole. Many people forget about support, but it is critical to a successful business. Once we've closed the sale, we've only begun the work with the customer. We have to ensure that the product continues to meet that customer's needs and that the customer gets top-level service. We see billions spent on software packages that end up staying on shelves because companies simply don't support them. The products themselves are wonderful but often difficult to use. It's a huge waste of money for the customer that will never come back and spend more money on the product. We need to build the relationship with the customer and address his or her needs. It's something I spend a lot of time working on and thinking about.

As intuitive as this sounds – offering customers top quality service and support—too many companies don't fulfill customer expectations. Having spent numerous years in the very unique technology boom in Silicon Valley, you see an enormous amount of tenacity in companies that continue to grow, and you also learn from the mistakes of those companies that are no longer around.

The attention to customers certainly pays off in the long run. One of our largest deals with a Fortune 500 organization started with a simple $5,000 sale to a group in this organization that was deploying wireless access for their sales team at tradeshows. By working closely with that customer and exceeding their expectations in customer service, we were recommended to a larger part of the company's business, it's internal IT organization. So, in essence, that small piece of business led to the largest sale in the company's history. You impress your customers, no matter how large or small the account, to grow those accounts to something larger.

Hypothetical Situations

Your company needs to increase revenues by 25 percent over the next year.

First, I would take a look at where the opportunities are for increased revenue. I don't want to be overly simplistic, but, if you want to grow your revenue, you have to sell more volume or increase prices. It is hard to increase the price of existing products. The trend is for prices to go down. To increase revenue, you need to have new products capable of solving problems in one year. If you don't have products in the pipeline now, you certainly won't be able to develop those in a year. You need distribution deals to sell products more efficiently and get them out faster to more customers. Finding the right partners allows you to make yourself more efficient. That way, you can take advantage of other companies' feet as well as your own

Your company needs to reduce expenses by 25 percent over the next year.

You have to take a look at cost structure and where you are spending your money right now. You have to figure out the value being derived. If you are an organization like our company, a real tech innovator, it is hard to cut expenses in R&D. If you do so, you could end up sacrificing the future of your organization and losing your market advantage. At this stage of our organization, I would look at reducing the time and energy it takes to sell an individual customer account. This would lower cost structure without touching the quality of product. The answer varies from company to company. You have to make a realistic assessment of where money is being spent.

You have just lost a key employee on your team; how do you go about making sure everything else is covered?

If you are thinking about that only after you lost the employee, it is too late. You don't want a company to be too dependent on any one individual at any level in the company. You never know when someone is going to get hit by a bus. If that unfortunate event were to occur, you wouldn't want your company to suffer in an irreparable way. A good, responsible manager will make sure not to put him or herself in that position. In an organization, you need to identify your most critical employees and make sure they remain happy and productive employees.

The budget for your company has just been increased by 25 percent.

If the budget were to increase by 25 percent, I would continue to do the same things, while identifying the opportunities in which to achieve the greatest return for the company. If the needs are greatest on the product side, invest there. If they are in sales and distribution, invest it there.

Worst-case scenario from a competitor's standpoint?

The worst-case scenario would be if a competitor or a couple of competitors potentially merged with a larger organization that dramatically expanded the capabilities of their products. We constantly look at the overall market landscape to ensure that we are looking at all the opportunities, actions and activities we possibly can.

Worst-case scenario from a partner's standpoint?

My personal worse case scenario is that a partner no longer proves reliable. When we are partnering with organizations, in particular resellers and partners that are representing our product, we are putting our brand and reputation in their hands. The worst case scenario is when that partner does not provide the same level of support as we would ourselves. Then our reputation is damaged. To avoid this, we work with partners as closely as possible, qualifying them to ensure we are working only with partners that have a very good reputation.

Worst nightmare that could happen to your company/team?

To prepare for your company's worst nightmare, it's not enough to keep your eye on your own company. You have to look at the overall market landscape. People talk about the Intel culture of paranoia, always looking at what the most potentially threatening moves in the market are. In doing so, you also think through what your response to that would be. Wherever possible, you implement those moves, not waiting for someone else to inflict them on you. That is a trap that a lot of small companies fall into. They focus on building their own product and don't pay enough attention to the market landscape, assuming the market landscape is going to remain static. In reality, it is going to be dynamic. You need a clear, competitive advantage. Your competitors may get nervous and try to regain the initiative, but a constant overall assessment of the competitive landscape is critical. You always have to put yourself in your competitor's shoes. If I were the competitor, what would I be doing to compete more effectively with AirWave? There will be few things that your competitors can think of that you haven't already thought of. You'll be in a much better position.

Keeping Your Edge

To stay on top of the market, there is nothing better than getting out there and talking to customers, hearing what they are talking about, the needs they are expressing. At the end of the day, they will determine if we are successful as a company. We need to stay abreast of the industry and look at all the information, building a network of contacts, people that are good sources of information. You also have to make sure that you don't get marred in the industry, talking to the same people all the time. It is necessary to talk to customers and understand what they are doing.

Customers, advisory councils, and distribution partners are all extremely valuable. There certainly are a lot of industry resources that are essential, including the press, but, at the end of the day, those resources are following the industry. Those that lead the industry are the people making the decisions of what to buy and what not to buy. We want to hear from them first.

Best Piece of Advice

The best piece of advice that I have received is to always be very, very honest. You also have to be careful in assessing products, the difference between a "nice-to-have product" and a "need-to-have product." Those that have not succeeded are involved in the "nice-to-have products," which may be necessary down the road but are not on the top three or four list of products that companies actually need at the moment.

Before you make a decision as to what is essential for customers, talk to them and have them tell you what is essential for them. If you are fighting to convince the customer, you are already behind. Once you've identified what the customer considers essential, you are in a position to help him or her and educate the customer in resolving his or her problem. That is particularly critical for small companies in a start-up environment. You don't have the luxury of sitting back and waiting for the world to need your product in three or four years. If this is the line of thinking, you aren't going to be around in three to four years.

There is also a lot to be said for persistence. One of the things a start-up company has to consider is whether the company should spend two years perfecting the product or simply get it out on the market as quickly as possible, even if that means upgrading it with additional features in the future. My bias is to get that product out quickly in order to get it into real customer hands. Small companies can do this much better than larger companies, who kick a product around in the lab before they bring it to the industry. Larger companies measure product release cycles in years, something small companies cannot afford to do.

Recent Changes

The industry is much larger and real in a way it has not always been in the past. The market has changed and customers, frankly, are a lot more skeptical than they used to be. We went through the hype cycle, and, now, customers are perhaps a little bit tired of vendors telling them just how essential their products are and what they are going to need in three to four years. Customers want to know what kind of value you can bring them today. There is a lot more realism. Customers are not willing to spend millions on speculative technology. Of course, this sometimes goes overboard, where customers aren't willing to try anything new. Sometimes the pendulum swings too far.

The Future

On the business side, I think prices will eventually decrease. Over time, there is usually a downward pressure on prices overall. I would characterize the wireless industry as being in the early stages. Right now, the pressure on most organizations is rapid innovation and solving problems for the customer, rather than on the commoditization pushing prices downward. But, in looking at history, as industries mature, the only way you are going to maintain and, eventually, increase prices is to deliver products that offer more value to customers.

In general, the wireless networking market is going to stop talking about wireless networking as a separate standalone industry. Wireless networks are part of an overall network. If you are a service provider, how do you integrate your wireless network with all your other tools? Wireless is going to be another way to connect to infrastructure. We are moving from having a standalone network to having an overall network. We can draw an analogy to 1999, where everyone was talking about the Internet as this amazing new and revolutionary technology. It was viewed as a standalone entity that organizations were going to use to communicate with, and sell to, their end users. Today, the Internet is another part of an overall strategy, not a separate standalone decision. I think that wireless is going to be part of an overall infrastructure, integrating with all the other tools in an organization.

Greg Murphy leads AirWave's business operations, backed by years of senior executive management experience in high-technology companies. Mr. Murphy joined AirWave from Idealab Silicon Valley, where he had been both an entrepreneur-in-residence from December 1999 and vice president of company development.

Previously, Mr. Murphy worked for On Command Corporation, the leading provider of in-room entertainment to the worldwide lodging industry. Mr. Murphy served as vice president of regional operations, with operational responsibility for systems generating over

$200 million in annual revenue. He also served as vice president of product management, guiding the launch of the lodging industry's first digital, interactive platform, providing video-on-demand, in-room Internet access and guest services.

Mr. Murphy built his high-tech experience with positions in programming and video operations within On Command. He earned his B.A. from Amherst College and his M.A. from Stanford University.

C-Level Quarterly Journal
What Every Executive Needs to Know

The Quarterly Journal Written by C-Level (CEO, CFO, CTO, CMO, Partner) Executives from the World's Top Companies

The objective of C-Level is to enable you to cover all your knowledge bases and be kept abreast of critical business information and strategies by the world's top executives. Each quarterly issue features articles on the core areas of which every executive must be aware, in order to stay one step ahead - including management, technology, marketing, finance, operations, ethics, law, hr and more. Over the course of the year, C-Level features the thinking of executives from over half the Global 500 and other leading companies of all types and sizes. While other business publications focus on the past, or current events, C-Level helps executives stay one step ahead of major business trends that are occurring 6 to 12 months from now.

Sample C-Level Executive Contributors/Subscribers Include:

Advanced Fibre Communications, Akin Gump Strauss Hauer & Feld, American Express, American Standard Companies, AmeriVest Properties, A.T. Kearney, AT&T Wireless, Bank of America, Barclays, BDO Seidman, BearingPoint (Formerly KPMG Consulting), BEA Systems, Bessemer Ventures, Best Buy, BMC Software, Boeing, Booz-Allen Hamilton, Boston Capital Ventures, Burson-Marsteller, Corning, Countrywide, Cravath, Swaine & Moore, Credit Suisse First Boston, Deutsche Bank, Dewey Ballantine, Duke Energy, Ernst & Young, FedEx, Fleishman-Hilliard, Ford Motor Co., General Electric, Hogan & Hartson, IBM, Interpublic Group, Jones, Day, Reavis & Pogue Ketchum, KPMG, LandAmerica, Leo Burnett, Mack-Cali Realty Corporation, Merrill Lynch, Micron Technology, Novell, Office Depot, Ogilvy & Mather, On Semiconductor, Oxford Health, PeopleSoft, Perot Systems, Prudential, Ropes & Gray, Saatchi & Saatchi, Salomon Smith Barney, Staples, TA Associates, Tellabs, The Coca-Cola Company, Unilever, Verizon, VoiceStream Wireless, Webster Financial Corporation, Weil, Gotshal & Manges, Yahoo!, Young & Rubicam

Subscribe & Become a Member of C-Level
Only $219.95/Year for 4 Quarterly Issues

Call 1-866-Aspatore or Visit www.Aspatore.com to Order

Management Best Sellers

Visit Your Local Bookseller Today or www.Aspatore.com For More Information

- Corporate Ethics - Making Sure You are in Compliance With Ethics Policies; How to Update/Develop an Ethics Plan for Your Team - $17.95

- 10 Technologies Every Executive Should Know - Executive Summaries of the 10 Most Important Technologies Shaping the Economy - $17.95

- The Board of the 21st Century - Board Members From Wal-Mart, Philip Morris, and More on Avoiding Liabilities and Achieving Success in the Boardroom - $27.95

- Inside the Minds: Leading CEOs - CEOs from Office Max, Duke Energy and More on Management, Leadership and Profiting in Any Economy - $27.95

- Deal Teams - Roles and Motivations of Management Team Members, Investment Bankers, Professional Services Firms, Lawyers and More in Doing Deals (Partnerships, M&A, Equity Investments) - $27.95

- The Governance Game - What Every Board Member and Corporate Director Should Know About What Went Wrong in Corporate America and What New Responsibilities They Are Faced With - $24.95

- Smart Business Growth - Leading CEOs on 12 Ways to Increase Revenues and Profits for Your Team/Company - $27.95

Buy All 7 Titles Above and Save 40 percent - Only $114.95

Call 1-866-Aspatore or Visit www.Aspatore.com to Order

Other Best Sellers

Visit Your Local Bookseller Today or www.Aspatore.com For A Complete Title List

- Ninety-Six and Too Busy to Die - Life Beyond the Age of Dying - $24.95

- Technology Blueprints - Strategies for Optimizing and Aligning Technology Strategy and Business - $69.95

- The CEO's Guide to Information Availability - Why Keeping People and Information Connected is Every Leader's New Priority - $27.95

- Being There Without Going There - Managing Teams Across Time Zones, Locations and Corporate Boundaries - $24.95

- Profitable Customer Relationships - CEOs from Leading Software Companies on using Technology to Maxmize Acquisition, Retention and Loyalty - $27.95

- The Entrepreneurial Problem Solver - Leading CEOs on How to Think Like an Entrepreneur and Solve Any Problem for Your Team/Company - $27.95

- The Philanthropic Executive - Establishing a Charitable Plan for Individuals and Businesses - $27.95

- The Golf Course Locator for Business Professionals - Organized by Closest to Largest 500 Companies, Cities and Airports - $12.95

- Living Longer Working Stronger - 7 Steps to Capitalizing on Better Health - $14.95

- Business Travel Bible - Must Have Phone Numbers, Business Resources, Maps and Emergency Info - $19.95

- ExecRecs - Executive Recommendations for the Best Business Products and Services Professionals Use to Excel - $14.95

Call 1-866-Aspatore or Visit www.Aspatore.com to Order